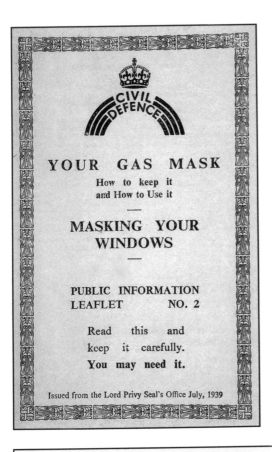

YOUR GAS MASK

How to keep it
and How to Use it

—

MASKING YOUR WINDOWS

—

PUBLIC INFORMATION
LEAFLET   NO. 2

Read   this   and
keep   it   carefully.
You may need it.

Issued from the Lord Privy Seal's Office July, 1939

I WISH TO MARK, BY THIS PERSONAL MESSAGE, my appreciation of the service you have rendered to your Country in 1939.

In the early days of the War you opened your door to strangers who were in need of shelter, & offered to share your home with them.

I know that to this unselfish task you have sacrificed much of your own comfort, & that it could not have been achieved without the loyal co-operation of all in your household.

By your sympathy you have earned the gratitude of those to whom you have shown hospitality, & by your readiness to serve you have helped the State in a work of great value.

Elizabeth R

Mrs. Brookhurst.

Henry Evenden,

Costumier, Mantle Maker, Outfitter,
General Draper, Glover, Laceman.

Telephone (Trunk) 23.
*

LONDON HOUSE,
FOOT OF DEVONSHIRE PLACE,
EASTBOURNE.

SOLE PROPRIETOR
OF THE CELEBRATED

Beachy Head Serge.

WEAR ABSOLUTELY GUARANTEED.

Houses Furnished throughout.   *Funeral and Mourning Orders executed,*

EASTBOURNE
A HISTORY

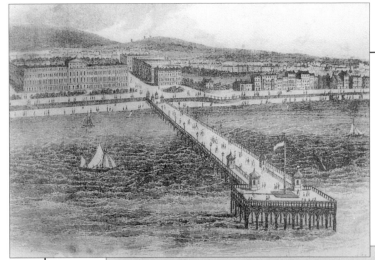

Eastbourne pier, which opened in 1870, had its landward half washed away in a storm in 1877. You can see today how the rebuilt part is at a slightly higher level then the far section. The bottom picture shows the pier in 1901 with the new theatre near the landing stage.

EASTBOURNE

A HISTORY

John Surtees

Phillimore

2002

Published by
PHILLIMORE & CO. LTD
Shopwyke Manor Barn, Chichester, West Sussex, England

ISBN 1 86077 226 9

Printed and bound in Great Britain by
BIDDLES LTD
Guildford, Surrey

Contents

List of Illustrations vii

Acknowledgements ix

1. The New Resort 1780-1850 1

2. Before the Royal Princes 19

3. Increased Prospects 1850-1900 35

4. Solid Respectability 1900-1938 61

5. The Most Bombed Town on the South Coast 96

6. Spotlight on a Changing Town 111

Notes and References 128

Index 131

List of Illustrations

Frontispiece: The pier before and after the storm of 1877

1.	The Great House	1
2.	Compton Place, 1785	2
3.	Map of Eastbourne, 1819	3
4.	Eastbourne beach	4
5.	Lady Elizabeth Compton	5
6.	Plan and lease of the barracks	5
7.	The Horse Barracks by F. Grose	6
8.	Martello towers	7
9.	Eastbourne's first theatre	7
10.	Militiaman's letter, 1808	8
11.	Burnt Cottage and smuggling	9
12.	Eastbourne's library	10
13.	Rose Cottage and the sheepwash	11
14.	The *Thames* stranded on the beach	12
15.	Old Town, 1840	13
16.	Jenny Lind, an early visitor	14
17.	Holy Trinity Church	15
18.	Eastbourne Parsonage Barn	15
19.	Marine Parade fishermen	16
20.	The first train 1849	17
21.	The *Gilbert Arms*	18
22.	Beachy Head flints and chalk	20
23.	Bronze-Age sickle	21
24.	Shaft in the chalk at Belle Tout	21
25.	Iron Age 'Waster' urn	21
26.	Plan of Roman Villa	22
27.	Roman flue tile	22
28.	Roman coin found at Beachy Head	23
29.	Saxon spear and brooches	23
30.	Motcombe and the Bourne stream	24
31.	The Jesus House	25
32.	Flint-built house	26
33.	Compton Place Lodge flintwork	27
34.	Wreck of the *Nympha Americana*	28
35.	Ceiling at Compton Place	29
36.	Smuggling seizure	30
37.	Mills of Eastbourne	31
38.	St Mary's Parish Church	32
39.	The Lushington Memorial	32
40.	Eastbourne's oldest house	33
41.	The Gilbert Manor House	34
42.	The *Lamb Inn*	34
43.	Artist's idea of the Grand Parade	35
44.	Devonshire Place and the Duke	36
45.	Cornfield Terrace	37
46.	The Princess Alice tree	38
47.	Eastbourne's oldest postbox	38
48.	The Vestry Hall	39
49.	Christ Church and Infants' School	40
50.	Meads Road, *c.*1895	40
51.	Diplock's off-licence today	41
52.	Frederick Gowland Hopkins PRS	41
53.	Eastbourne front	42
54.	The 1867 Langney sewer	43
55.	View from St Saviour's spire	44
56.	Araluen, later *Cumberland Hotel*	45
57.	Union Workhouse, *c.*1890	46
58.	1836 school in Meads Road	46
59.	All Saints' Hospital, *c.*1895	47
60.	Garden of de Walden House	48
61.	The Duke's Orchestra	49
62.	*Grand Hotel,* 1890	50
63.	Princess Alice Hospital opening	51
64.	The Town Hall	53
65.	Eastbourne station, *c.*1890	54
66.	Salvation Army riots	55
67.	Lewis Carroll's lodging	56
68.	Licence Plates	56
69.	The Minstrels	57
70.	Eastbourne's lifeboats	58
71.	Bathing on the Sands	59
72.	Bathing, *c.*1900	59
73.	*York House Hotel, c.*1905	60
74.	Building the lighthouse	62
75.	Beachy Head, *c.*1910	62
76.	The promenade, 1912	63
77.	A visit by King Edward VII	64
78.	Caffyn's Garage, 1904	64
79.	A 1904 bus at Ocklynge	65
80.	Seaside Baths and Library	66
81.	The Technical Institute, 1904	67
82.	Staff of the Fever Hospital, 1902	68
83.	The Links, Meads	68
84.	The pool at St Cyprian's School	69

85. A Pierrot troupe 70
86. Bernard Fowler and his wife 71
87. Cabmen's shelter 72
88. Rupert Brooke 73
89. Louis G. Ford's first shop, 1912 74
90. Airplane built at Eastbourne 75
91. Upperton Red Cross Hospital 76
92. Summerdown Camp 77
93. Caffyn-made plane fragment 79
94. Central Military Hospital, 1917 79
95. Unveiling of War Memorial 81
96. The Bungalow Stores 82
97. The Age of Jazz 83
98. Site of Emily Kaye's murder 84
99. Hampden Park, 1922 85
100. Charles Montagu Doughty 86
101. Downs Commemorative Seat 87
102. Thatched telephone box 88
103. Shop display, c.1925 88
104. Fishermen's catch 89
105. Visit from the Graf Zeppelin 90
106. Amy Johnson's plane 91
107. Prince of Wales' visit 91
108. PS Brighton Queen 92
109. The new bandstand 92
110. Allchorn pleasure boats 93
111. Coronation celebrations 1937 94
112. Eastbourne Police Force 1938 95
113. SS Barnhill on fire 97
114. Dunkirk survivors 98
115. Eastbourne Home Guard 99
116. Eastbourne's first bomb 99
117. Me110 shot down 100
118. Shelled by a U-boat 100
119. Christ Church School burnt out 100
120. Latimer Road blast effects 101
121. Cavendish Place rescue, 1940 101
122. Bobby's bombed 102
123. Unexploded bomb removal 103
124. German TV test card 104
125. Shot-up bus 105
126. The Marks & Spencer's bomb site 106
127. Nurses in tin hats 107
128. Bomb Alley, January 1943 107
129. Grove Road, 4 June 1943 108
130. Bouncing bomb 109
131. A doodlebug over the cliffs 109
132. Astaire Avenue meets a V1 109
133. Caffyn's keep going 110
134. Memorial Houses 111
135. The crowded front in the 1950s 112
136. Compton Place in the 1950s 113
137. The Birds Eye factory at Langney 114
138. The Crumbles tramway 116
139. Redoubt Model Village 116
140. Germania stranded at Cow Gap 117
141. Sunderland flying boat crash 117
142. Frederick Soddy FRS 118
143. Dr Bodkin Adams 118
144. Train crash, 1958 119
145. Wish Tower café and lounge 120
146. The Congress Theatre 120
147. South Cliff Tower 121
148. Central Library, 1946-64 121
149. Eastbourne floral display 122
150. Flats along Upperton Road 123
151. 'Eastbourne Corporation' 123
152. School memorial arch 124
153. Arndale Centre before and after 124
154. Devonshire Park Theatre 125
155. A 1989 visit by Princess Diana 126
156. Devonshire Park tennis 126
157. Restoration of c.1790 hermitage 127
158. 'Airbourne 2000' 127

Acknowledgements

My special thanks go to my wife, Sheila, for her help and encouragement. Acknowledgements to Brian Allchorn, Stanley Apps, David Arscott, D. Barker, Ken Batham, A.D. Baxter, Clive Beck, Dr J.J. Bending, Steve Benz, Wilf Bignell, Alex Bransgrove, Judith Brent, Stephen Brewer, Ann & Alan Caffyn, Richard Callaghan, John Cant, George Catt, Muriel Childs, Mavis Clack, John V. Claremont, Gordon Clark, Michael Clark, E. Venn Claydon, Betty & Arthur Cobb, Terry Connolly, M.J. Cruttenden, Owen Daish, J. & L. Davies-Gilbert, W.H. Day, Harry C. Deal, John Dow, Peter L. Drewett, Dorothy Ecroyd, Bob Elliston, A.G.S. Enser, John Farrant, Ian H. Ford, Lawrence Ford, Paul E. Fulford, Eric Gates, Denys Giddey, Richard Gilbert, Frank Glyn-Jones, John Gowland, Alastair Graham, Clive Griggs, Stella Hardwick, Paul Harris, Ken Harrison, Vida Herbison, F.G. Heys, Ted Hide, G.R. Hodges, Vera Hodsoll, Maureen Honey, Graham Household, Chris Howden, Roy Hudson, Frances Jardine, George Jones, Lionel Jones, Melanie Jones, Derek Keay, W.H. Kefford, Harold C. & Sylvia Kennedy, Lorna Kenward, David Kingsley, Dr N.A. Kinniburgh, Margaret T. Knight, Pat Lambie, Percy G. Langdon, Anna Langton, Dr A.M. Lester, Jane Leete, Marie Lewis, Peter Longstaff-Tyrrell, S.F. Lott, Lou McMahon, Harry Margary, Pauline Markquick, John Martin, Rosemary & John Milton, Frances Muncey, Michael Ockenden, Dr J.D. O'Connor, Liz Oliver-Taylor, Miriam C. Nixey, Betty & Peter Palmer, Hugh Parker, Ron & Elsie Parsons, Michael Partridge, Lisa Pickard, Roy Porter, Hilary & Ron Pringle, Jack Putland, Nigel Quiney, John Redfern, Brian Robinson, Sheila & Ken Sargeant, Mary & Tom Searle, P. Short, Mike Sibson, Cheryl Smith, Laurence Snowball, Harold D. Spears, John & Irene Stevens, Pat & Lawrence Stevens, R.G. Stewart, D. Swift, Gillian Tarrant, Nick Taylor, Joan & Ken Thurman, Doreen Toghill, Luisa Tomasetti, C. Tonge, Betty Turner, Ronald Turner, Dr K.O.A. Vickery, W.J. Vine, Pauline Wade, Debbie Wall, Jack Warne, Kate Watson, Derek Wilkinson, Edgar Williams, Iris K. Wilson, Cecille Woodford, Esther Worsfold, Pam Young.

Beckett Publications, British Library, British Museum, Caffyn's plc. publicity department, University Library Cambridge, Channel Photography, Eastbourne Local History Society, Eastbourne Town Council minutes, Eastbourne Central Library, Eastbourne Natural History and Archaeological Society, East Sussex Record Office, Hastings Museum, Walter Llewellyn & Sons Ltd., Museum of History of Science Oxford University, National Portrait Gallery, Phillimore & Co., Towner Art Gallery and History Museum.

Whilst every effort has been made to contact all relevant individuals and organisations, it is regretted that it has not been possible to locate them all. Those left out are asked to accept the author's apologies.

One

The New Resort 1780-1850

The story of Eastbourne's transformation from a few hamlets on the brink of treacherous waters to the Empress of Watering Places begins in 1780. Brighton had Dr Richard Russell to thank for its start, Hastings had James Burton, but for select Eastbourne it could only be the Royal Princes.

The Princes, and Princesses, the youngest children of King George III and Queen Charlotte, stayed from June to October at Seahouses, just to the east of the present pier. Their coaches were given a right royal welcome 'by the Riding Officers and Tradesmen of the place and were received by a discharge of Mr. Willard's cannon'.[1] Lady Charlotte Finch and her charges would have found Eastbourne quiet – apart from Mr Willard's cannon – but blessed with plenty to do. 'From Bourne you go through a long street South-Bourne, and Shady Lane [Trinity Trees] with trees and hedges to Sea-Houses beach,

1 The Great House, Seahouses, where the Princesses Elizabeth, 10, and Sophia, three, stayed in 1780 with the baby, Prince Octavius, the King's 13th child, but eighth son. Prince Edward, aged 12, was with his tutors in the Round House, an old mill near today's pier. He became Duke of Kent and father of Queen Victoria. Lady Charlotte Finch, governess, was at New Susans.

1

2 Compton Place (seen here in 1783), was Bourne Place until bought by Spencer Compton. There was no question of the royal party staying at Compton Place because the owner, Lady Elizabeth Compton, was an unmarried woman of 20, her parents having died of tuberculosis, and she lived with the Duchess of Beaufort, her grandmother. As she was not in residence, however, the royals were able to visit her house and grounds.

where you enjoy sea air, bathing, the sands, sailing, shooting, hunting, walking and riding.'[2]

The royal children bathed in the sea or at Mrs Mary Webb's new Warm Sea Water Baths, where the Leaf Hall is now. They walked on the beach, visited Compton Place, and had lessons. They also went to nearby East Dean, Birling Gap, and Herstmonceux and Pevensey Castles. Robert Gibbs, the Compton Place bailiff, wrote, '... every house is full and if ever this becomes a public place it will be more due to the Royal Children ... than any other thing'.[3] One of the diaries reads, '17 July 1780. After Princess Elizabeth and Princess Sophia have bathed, we walk on the sands. At nine o'clock, after breakfast, we go to Lady Charlotte Finch's lodgings and she goes with us to Compton Place. We stay an hour and Lady CF accompanies Princess Elizabeth to the Round-House ... for various lessons. Lady CF returns at three when Prince Edward, his tutor, Mr. Bruyéres, sub-tutor, Mr.

Farhill, and the Revd. Fisher come to dinner. HRH and the gentlemen leave at five.'[4] John Fisher, Chaplain to the Bishop Preceptor and principal overseer of Prince Edward's education, accompanied the royal party to Eastbourne, where he arranged sketching for the older children. It has no significance whatsoever in the choice of Eastbourne for the holiday, but members of his family were vicars of Eastbourne from 1779 to 1805.

The royal visit was at the instigation of James Royer, a Court Treasury official who had built New Susans (now Elms Avenue) as his Eastbourne house close to Susans Farmhouse, from which we derive Susans Road. He also published the first *Guide to Eastbourne* in 1787, which described 'the various beautiful prospects and diversified scenes of this healthy and romantic spot'. The combination of royalty, religion, money, beauty, romance and health couldn't be beaten by any holiday brochure of today. Since then Eastbourne has had its

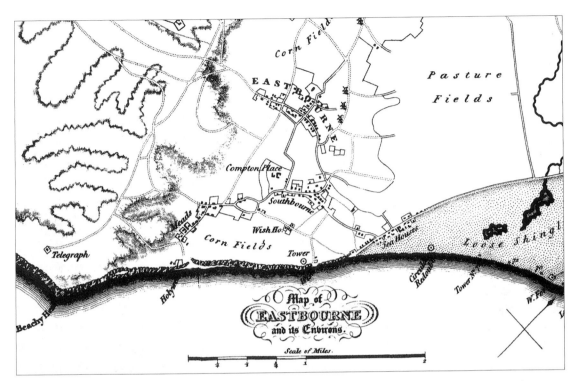

3 Heatherly's map of 1819 shows a group of four tiny hamlets that had hardly changed for a thousand years. The first census of 1801 boasted only 1,668 inhabitants. There was Old Town, or Borne ('Eastbourne' here), with St Mary's parish church, the *Lamb Inn*, the Gilbert Manor House and a huddle of cottages at the old Saxon crossroads; Southbourne, with its sheepwash, a hamlet near the present railway station; and 'Sea Houses'. To the west was the farming homestead of Meads.

moments, but has never looked back. Another Royal, Princess Amelia, visited the town in 1789 and 1790, so the stay of 1780 must have been a great success.

Sea bathing developed from the practice of touring curative spas. Medical opinion advocated sea bathing to 'preserve health and cure many diseases', and by 1735 coastal spas, such as Scarborough, were becoming popular. Dr Russell's dissertation of 1752 established the fashion for bathing along the south coast, although he advocated *drinking* sea water; it was understood that bathing was beneficial, not pleasurable. Men bathed naked until Victorian times when stockinette costumes made an entrance, 'covering but never concealing the bather's fair form', and segregated bathing lasted into the 20th century.[5]

A private school 'for the sons of gentlemen' was next required, and The Gables in Church Street (on the Edgmond Hall car park) opened in 1790 and ran

until 1902, with a curriculum described as 'very little history or geography, but plenty of Latin and Greek. The food was terrible, dinner consisted of two courses, jam or treacle pudding first and meat afterwards, so that the boys would not eat too much of the more expensive meat'.[6] In the 1790s there was already a building where Fairfield Road is now, and from 1816 it was called Southfield Lodge, or Southfields, and in 1841 was enlarged.[7] Renamed St Winifred's, it became a girls' school in 1880 and is now Southfields Lodge a block of luxury flats.

Among the new visitors were French courtesans who landed on the beach as refugees from the guillotine, thereby involving Eastbourne in the turmoil of the French Revolution. On one day in September 1792 300 émigrés put ashore here to escape the Reign of Terror. In February 1793 France declared war on England and Holland, and that summer a survey party selected Beachy Head as a suitable site for a wartime signal station. The

4 Bathing huts *c.*1873. Present on the Seahouses beach from about 1760, these were subsequently stationed between the old bandstand and the Wish Tower, with separate sections for males and females. They were pulled into and out of the water by horses, with fearsome women, 'Dippers', on hand to encourage the timid and assist the sick. Made static after the First World War, their final heroic stand was as invasion barricades in 1940.

war was to drag on and off for over twenty years, and demanded a round-the-year watch along the south coast in case of invasion. One mad Frenchman even proposed to attack *via* a tunnel under the Channel.

Since the time of William III troops had been billeted in inns or camps to avoid hardship to ordinary people, but the influx of troops meant that many were under canvas, where they suffered in the winter, or brought an increasingly unprofitable burden to the innkeepers of Sussex. Prime Minister William Pitt had little choice but to build winter quarters. The *Sussex Weekly Advertiser* [*SWA*] of 2 June 1794 has mention of a barracks, and Ann Hudson states, 'July, Cavalry barracks for 54 men ordered and preparing to build', but a lease dated 16 December 1794 is the earliest local documentary evidence for a building.[8] Other barracks were erected east of the town in Langney,

and in 1795 the East and West Langney Forts were constructed on a low bar of shingle, the Crumbles.

Inevitably, the influx of strangers was not always smooth. The *SWA* of 10 June 1793 reported that two robbers had broken into a lodging house called the Round House at Eastbourne, the property of Miss Mortimer, and stolen two beds. On 22 July at the Lewes Assizes two Surrey Militiamen were convicted of the crime and sentenced to seven years' transportation. In 1802 the three lords of the manor of Eastbourne, Lord George Cavendish, Charles Gilbert and Inigo Thomas, leased an area of shingle to the Board of Ordnance; this is the present TA Ordnance Yard in Seaside. There is an incised block at the junction of Cambridge Road and Seaside that could be an original boundary marker.

When invasion was imminent, in 1803, a count was taken of all livestock and persons, and plans for evacuation were drawn up. These Lieutenancy

5 Lady Elizabeth Compton Peters (1760-1835), a descendant of Spencer Compton and only child of the Earl of Northampton. Her marriage to Lord George Augustus Henry Cavendish, a younger son of the 4th Duke of Devonshire, on 27 February 1782, was momentous for Eastbourne. It brought her Sussex estates to the Cavendishes. The couple's line were not expected to inherit the title, but a grandchild, William, 2nd Earl of Burlington, became the 7th Duke, and transformed the four hamlets into Eastbourne.

6 Part of the Figg Map of *c*.1816 showing 'Horse Barracks plot 34'. The purchase of the land is in a lease of 1794: 'all that copyhold parcel of ground containing 4 acres more or less … on the public road from Eastbourne up the hill and reputed to be part of Dyers Farm which was leased by Nicholas Gilbert to the use of the Rt. Hon. William Wyndham in trust for the King's Majesty at a yearly rent of £1 16s.' William Wyndham was the War Minister, and the 'parcel of ground' is now Letheren Place on the A259 road from Eastbourne up the hill to Brighton.

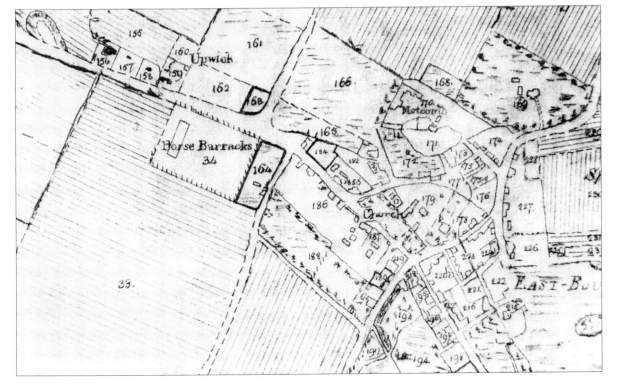

7 Most barracks were of timber construction on brick foundations, but the Eastbourne Old Town barracks was for dragoons and the horses deserved something better. Consequently a substantial two-storey brick building appeared. In 1817 it became the poor house, in 1835 the workhouse, and in 1930 St Mary's Hospital. Drawn by Francis Grose, soldier son of the antiquary, c.1795, the view is from around Upland Road, with St Mary's Church tower to the left. The little building with a chimney is the farrier's shop.

Records show that Eastbourne had 7,173 sheep, 356 pigs, 351 cattle, 186 horses, 172 oxen, and one goat, that the town could produce 66 volunteers armed with four swords, 65 firearms and 55 pitchforks, and each miller could produce some two sacks of flour a day. The Records also showed that there were insufficient wagons for an evacuation so that was shelved.[9] Home defence was partly in the hands of militias raised around the country but a military presence boosted the size and importance of Eastbourne. In 1804 it was reported that, 'in spite of the menace of the enemy, this little watering place has to boast of its fullest season ever known'.[10]

An engineer, Captain W.H. Ford, drew up plans for the defence of the south coast in 1804, and in the spring of the following year Brigadier-General W. Twiss, an expert in defence works, rode into Eastbourne to select the Martello tower sites.[11] In April 1805 the *SWA* reported that work had begun on the Martello towers 'to protect the exposed coast', and on 9 September, 'Mr. Pitt and Lord Castlereagh were on Tuesday at Eastbourne … and viewed with attention the Martello Tower erecting there'. They were built between 1805 and 1812, although the threat of invasion ceased

after August 1805, when Napoleon broke camp at Boulogne to deal with Austria.

Only six remain of the towers built to provide covering fire over the low ground between Pevensey Bay and Beachy Head. Number 55 is still at Norman's Bay, 56-59 have been demolished or fallen into the sea, 60 survives, 61 is in the Martello estate, 62 is in a caravan site, 63 was destroyed by enemy action during the Second World War, 64 is in the sea, 65 has collapsed, and 66 is near the new Sovereign Harbour. The one on St Anthony's Hill, 68, was demolished for housing, although the site can be discerned by the arrangement of the roads, and 67 and 69-72 have been demolished or fallen into the sea. Number 73, on the Eastbourne sea-front opposite Wilmington Square, is known as the Wish Tower. Built on a greensand outcrop, it owes its name to the marshy land, The Wish, near the seafront. The Great Redoubt Fortress in Royal Parade was built about the same time to house 350 men and 11 guns, but it is doubtful if more than 200 were ever accommodated. It acted as a fort and depôt for the Martello towers.[12]

The lessening of the threat of invasion was apparent when, on 27 September 1805, the Duke of Cumberland felt free to review his troops on

8 The Martello towers were named after a tower on Mortella Point in Corsica, whose stout resistance in 1793 impressed Admiral Jervis. They ran from near Folkestone in Kent to No.74 at Seaford. The well-constructed squat towers, like upturned flowerpots from a distance, were a force to be reckoned with in their day, with their robust walls, a ditch, and a gun on the roof, the smallest being 24-pounders. They provided years of work for local builders.

9 The South Street Theatre was Eastbourne's first, built for the Fisher family in 1798. It lay almost opposite today's *Dewdrop Inn*. When the troops left demand fell off and it was taken over as a carpenter's shop by the Haine family in 1838. It was demolished in the 1880s, by which time Haine's business had moved over the road.

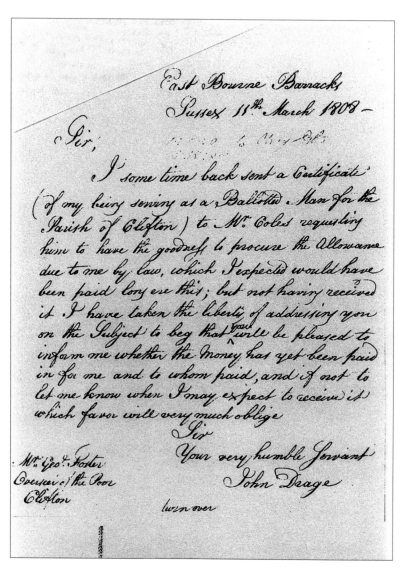

East Bourne Barracks
Sussex 11th March 1808 –

Sir,

I some time back sent a Certificate
(of my being serving as a Balloted Man for the
Parish of Clifton) to Mr Coles requesting
him to have the goodness to procure the Allowance
due to me by law, which I expected would have
been paid long ere this; but not having received
it I have taken the liberty of addressing you
on the Subject to beg that you will be pleased to
inform me whether the Money has yet been paid
in for me and to whom paid, and if not to
let me know when I may expect to receive it
which favor will very much oblige
Sir
Your very humble Servant
John Drage

Mr Geo't Foster
Overseer of the Poor
Clifton

turn over

10 A militiaman's letter from Eastbourne barracks, 11 March 1808. The militia were chosen by lot, but you could pay someone to go in your place if you were sufficiently wealthy. With Lt.-General Sir James Pulteney in command, detachments of the 10th and 11th Dragoons, and the Sussex and South Gloucester Militia, under George, 4th Lord Dynevor, were in the town. At varying times the Dorset, North Hants, Glamorgan and South Herts Militia were on Beachy Head.

Beachy Head. Nelson's victory at Trafalgar the next month removed all danger to Britain, and soon troops were taking the war to the French on the continent. Not without losses, inevitably, and Major the Hon. George Cavendish, son of Lord George Henry Cavendish and Lady Elizabeth Compton Peters, was lost at sea returning from the Corunna evacuation in January 1809.

During all these momentous happenings everyday life went on in the town. In March 1807 Captain Henry Goldfinch wrote to the Board of Ordnance, 'Within a short distance of the Ordnance office are some deposits of filth, such as the cleaning of necessaries, and slaughter houses in an open field immediately on the side of the road – the nuisance you may imagine in the hot season is excessive ...'. Eastbourne had been made a Post Town by 1797, letters beforehand having had to be sent to Lewes to join the General Post. The place for their receipt and dispatch was in Old Town, and on 27 April 1806 Thomas How was appointed the first sub-postmaster, working from Ocklynge Road. His wife succeeded to the post on his death in 1821.

The Rev. Dr Alexander Brodie, a scion of a Scottish family from Nairnshire who had made their money in Antigua, was instituted as vicar of

11 Burnt Cottage, on East Dean Road, was said to be a secret store for smugglers and burnt down by the Preventive Officers. The story goes that local people rebuilt it in 1830 to show their support for the smugglers. The Wish Tower and nearby Wish Hut were occupied by coastguards from 1831 to 1851. Most of the nearby smuggling was at Pevensey or Crowlink, but the last serious affray was at Eastbourne on 23 January 1833. A coastguard at the Wish Hut raised the alarm, but in the skirmish that ensued the smugglers shot and killed coastguard George Pett and ran the cargo through, taking any casualties with them.

Eastbourne in 1809 and at once pushed for a better parish poor school than the schoolroom at St Mary's parish church. This was Eastbourne's earliest school, although the first schoolmaster in the village dates back to 1586. In 1811 Brodie pulled down the schoolroom and the pupils were moved to a hired hall, but three years went by before he was able to persuade the lords of the manor to buy a plot of land opposite the church and become trustees of a new St Mary's Church of England National School. The Gilbert family added a floor in 1816 enabling girls to be taught upstairs. The building became St Mary's Girls' School, and a Girls' Council School in 1952, until demolition. The site is now an open space, part of St Mary's Court, but the pupils moved to Ocklynge Junior

School in Victoria Drive, where the old school bell is kept.

The Rev. Brodie bought the Gore Farmhouse in 1810, 'Gore' meaning a triangular piece of land. The family weren't short of money and they added to the house, extended the grounds, and lived there until 1892. The site gave its name to Gore Park Avenue and Road. Until 1810 St Mary's Church was the only place of worship in the town, but open-air services were held near Seahouses for Methodists in the militia, and a plot of land was acquired in 1809 from Mr. Willard for £145. The town's first non-conformist chapel opened on 28 March 1810 beside a trackway, which is now Grove Road.

Distinguished visitors were beginning to replace the army, and although not yet in sufficient numbers

12 John Heatherly took over 'George Fisher's Library and Lounge'. Eastbourne's first library, at 16/17 Marine Parade, opened for holiday visitors in 1784. It lasted, with its two upper bay windows, until 1948, when it was demolished having been damaged during the war.

to compensate financially, they were welcome. William Wilberforce enjoyed a break with his family in 1808, the year after the success of his anti-slavery campaign in Britain, while Charles Lamb, the essayist, had an off-day when he visited the town and called it 'dullest Eastbourne'. About this time Jane Austen set Eastbourne as the location for her novel, *Sanditon*.

Smuggling had peaked with the military commitments of the French wars and firmer measures were now needed to control it. The Preventive Waterguard, an inshore force, was introduced in 1809 to support the Customs and Excise Services in the control of smuggling, and at Eastbourne they had a station west of the Redoubt with a boat and watch house. The Waterguard was superseded by the Coast Blockade, a naval force hand-picked to combat smuggling. Stations were established in 1818 along parts of the Kent and Sussex coast as far

westwards as Seaford Head. The Eastbourne Watch House, together with a warehouse and boathouse, was built in 1819 on the shingle near the south-west corner of the Ordnance Yard.

There are records of 300 smugglers gathering for a landing at Crowlink in 1822, but the Coast Blockade was effective. In 1824 it was extended to cover the entire Sussex coast, and seven men from Eastbourne were transported for smuggling in 1828. The Coast Blockade was abolished in March 1831 and the Coastguard took over as an anti-smuggling force, as well as assisting in life-saving and helping at rescues. The Coastguard used the Watch House as accommodation for the Chief Officer and family, until it became unusable after a storm in 1857. This station moved to Hurst's Cottages, then Addingham Road, and eventually Wartling Road. Coastguard stations were also established at Martello towers 53, 55, 57, 62 and Langney Fort East, and

13 Pencil drawing by John Graham of Rose Cottage *c.*1825. To the left is the Bourne Stream and the sheepwash, which was in front and to the side of the present Central Library.

at Holywell, Birling Gap, Crowlink and Cuckmere Haven.[13]

With changes in the tax laws, smuggling was no longer profitable and large-scale runs had to wait for more recent times for revival. The siting and importance of the Coastguard stations altered during the 19th century, and in the 1880s Beachy Head station, hitherto a detachment of Birling Gap, took over in strategic importance from Holywell.

As soon as Napoleon was safely in St Helena the Dragoon Barracks was sold off to local land-owners and in 1817 leased to the Eastbourne overseers of the poor for use as a parish poor house. The barracks buildings to the east of the town were demolished between 1818 and 1823. The soldiers were swiftly demobbed and, with no trade, became a heavy charge on their parish, so that ratepayers believed the only way to bring down the taxes, which soared in the 1820s, was

to introduce 'reforms'. The Poor Law Amend-ment Act of 1834 was the outcome, and resulted in the Eastbourne Union workhouse.

In contrast, Eastbourne-by-the-Sea was doing well. By 1817 the library was run by John Heatherly, remarkable for his black suit, knee breeches, silk stockings and powdered hair. In his guidebook of 1819, *A description of Eastbourne and its environs*, he describes it as 'a good library, delightfully situated facing the sea, with one of the best lodging houses above, daily papers each day and periodical publications. The Library is very spacious, and in the adjoining room is an excellent Billiard Table kept quite select for the use of gentlemen only.' Heatherly ran the library and a shop until his death in 1839, and his widow and nieces, the Misses Lay, continued to 1845 after which the Misses Hopkins kept the shop for another 12 years. In 1824 Dr Brodie wrote, 'Eastbourne is

14   The well-publicised beaching in 1822 of the East Indiaman *Thames* after it hit rocks off Beachy Head led to the building of the Belle Tout lighthouse. 'Mad Jack Fuller' (1757-1834) of Rose Hill, Brightling, Lord Lieutenant of the County, mentor of J.M.W. Turner, and builder of follies, paid for the 1828-34 wooden Belle Tout lighthouse. It was superseded by the Trinity House one built of Aberdeen granite blocks.

as full as it can well hold ...', and by now the Assembly House in Seaside provided a small meeting room. A new peal of bells was installed in the parish church, the first peal being rung by the Brighton Society of Change Ringers on 26 October 1818; they are the bells we hear today. The £450 bill wasn't paid until 1820. 'Mad Jack Fuller' provided the funds for Eastbourne's first lifeboat, a 25ft. rowing boat of ten oars. The lifeboat station was established in 1822, next in line after Newhaven along the south coast, and two years before the national institution. Fuller might have been eccentric, but as a politician he knew the value of publicity, and when his lifeboat made its first rescue he had a medal struck displaying his name and bust. The Rev. Dr Brodie died in 1828 after being thrown out of his carriage in Ocklynge. His wife Anna was the daughter of John Walter, the founder of *The Daily Universal Examiner* or

The Times, and over the 19th century their children did a great deal of good work in the town.

Nicholas and Mary Gilbert's grandchildren both died childless in 1816, and the 'Gildredge/Gilbert' manor passed to their niece Mary Ann Gilbert. In 1808 she married Davies Giddy, MP, PRS, who changed his name to Davies Gilbert. Another large family was that of Inigo Freeman (later Freeman Thomas, to conform to his father-in-law's will) of Ratton Manor, who had 14 children. His second wife was Lady Frances Brodrick. He added two wings to the house, and the Upper Plantation was created for Lady Frances to view from her boudoir. In 1830 he sold his rights to the Crumbles, as well as his Eastbourne-Parker third interest in the Manor of Eastbourne, to the other manorial lords, the Cavendishes (Dukes of Devonshire) and the Davies Gilberts. By 1840 two-thirds of the parish, or 2,600 acres, was in Cavendish hands.[14]

15 Old Town in 1840. St Mary's Church is left centre, with the block of the workhouse (the old barracks) to the left. In the early 1800s Eastbourne orphans were sent to work in northern cotton mills, and around 1840 at least 50 residents 'were emigrated' to the Antipodes on a free passage. The main concern was to shift them out so that they were not a liability on the parish. Before long it was only the infirm, or those advanced in age, or those in a distressed state following the death of a breadwinner, who allowed themselves to be admitted to the workhouse.

The Eastbourne Union workhouse opened in March 1835 at the old Cavalry Barracks in Church Street. One aim of the 1834 Act was to aggregate the parish poorhouses into union workhouses, in the case of Eastbourne for 14 parishes from Seaford to Pevensey. The costs and resources of each parish had varied enormously but, unfortunately, the main intention wasn't to spread the load, but to present an uninviting aspect and thus deter applicants for relief. The harsh regime was soon in evidence: on 11 September 1835 the master punished Henry Collins, George Hatfield and Samuel Collins by keeping them on bread and water 'for such number of days he may think necessary'.

The regulations included strict separation of married men and women, which was bitterly resented by the poor. On 20 November 1835 George Whiteman, Clerk to the Guardians, wrote, '… a great disturbance in the Eastbourne workhouse. The married persons in the house appear to have conspired to prevent the separation of man and wife. The conduct of the parties has been most desperate. Fortunately … the Guardians have (by force) succeeded in getting two of the worst characters (men) into the blackhole, but the house continues in great confusion.'[15] When, in December 1835, the Guardians were accused by ratepayers of spoiling the inmates they replied that the diet was inferior to that of the labouring classes in the neighbourhood, and that 'the beer is of a very indifferent quality, indeed little better than water'.[16]

For a few years there was a workhouse school at Seaford, as part of the Eastbourne Union, and a letter expresses a sentiment typical of the times: 'this Board still entertain the opinion that the children in the Seaford School House should not be taught to write as they would otherwise be in a better situation than the children of a considerable

16 Johanna Maria (Jenny) Lind (1820-87). The 'Swedish Nightingale' occupied Cliff Cottage on two separate occasions around 1840. The cottage was a one-storey stone building which stood near today's Lascelles Terrace. She was frequently seen on the beach and was 'most affable'. Another holidaymaker was Alfred, Lord Tennyson (1809-92): he stayed at Eastbourne in 1843 and 1845, occupying Mount Pleasant, near the present *Cavendish Hotel*, for one season, and 22 Seahouses, near the *Albion Hotel* (now the *Carlton*) for the other.

number of the independent Agricultural Labourers in this Union'.[17] There is no doubt that poor relief costs were capped: in Sussex they fell from £262,735 in 1834-5 to £205,335 the next year, but at what cost to human dignity? Charles Dickens, who created Mr Bumble, the workhouse master in *Oliver Twist*, wrote, '… few anomalies in England are so horrible that the poor should creep in corners to die rather than fester and rot in such infamous places'. A lease of 24 December 1846 confirmed that the Guardians paid rent at £148 a year to the Earl of Burlington and John Davies Gilbert.

Otherwise, Eastbourne continued to attract the better class of tourist. In 1831 Dickens himself came to see Augustus Egg, the artist, who had rented

Pilgrims, the oldest house in Eastbourne, and Holman Hunt was said to be a later visitor. The town appeared once more in print. Theodore Edward Hook, who started the journal *John Bull*, had a character in his book *Jack Brag* (1836) amuse himself at Eastbourne by 'strolling on the sands, watching girls and throwing stones into the sea', all there was to do, for Eastbourne had stagnated since 1815. James Berry Morris wrote, 'In 1836 I journeyed from Lewes to Eastbourne in an old rumbling van occupying four hours on the road to spend my summer holidays. The *Albion* was being completed at the time. Further to the east was the Chief Coastguard Officer's house. One night the sea encroached and the family had to beat a retreat.'

17 Holy Trinity Church, now in Trinity Trees. In his appeal for funds the Rev. Thomas Pitman stated that the cost would be about £2,500 and that, of the 540 seats, half were to be free and for the use of the poor. Designed by Decimus Burton and consecrated on 8 December 1838 by Dr Otter, Bishop of Chichester, it became a parish church in 1847. It has been enlarged and altered, and the iron screens were brought from the demolished church of St Peter, Meads in 1973.

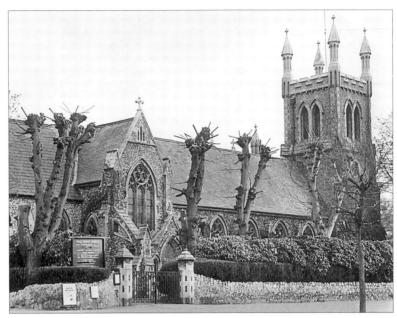

18 The farmyard of Rectory Manor or Parsonage farmhouse, next to St Mary's Church. Parsonage Barn is the main building, and to the left, behind the open-sided wagon store, was the Tithe Barn.

19 Marine Parade *c.*1860. The fishing boats were run onto the shingle beach near the *Albion Hotel*. The lifeboat hut is almost below the spire. The *Bee*, a typical collier, discharged opposite St Aubyn's Road. She also ran up the beach at high tide and was held fast by a warp from a capstan, while the coal was unloaded into wide-wheeled carts, often pulled by donkeys. As she had to pay every time a capstan was used, and for any storage of cargo on the beach, and for the light at the Customs House, the aim was to unload, ballast-up and float off with the next tide. The ballast was often flints, with timber if the coal had been for Heathfield.

The Rev. Thomas Pitman, who had succeeded the Rev. Brodie in 1828, realised there was a need for a church nearer the seaside and the Earl of Burlington was persuaded to donate a site. Pitman himself raised the money for the Eastbourne chapel of ease, later Holy Trinity Church.

Coal was brought to Eastbourne by collier brigs in vessels of 50-100 tons, with names such as *Bee*, *Collingwood*, *Pelican*, *Tally Ho* and *Tryall*, which were notoriously unseaworthy. They were at their peak about 1850 but trade fell off with competition from the railways; a few continued into the 1880s. The fishermen were also feeling the loss of their smuggling income and in 1839, after two poor fishing years, there was a collection to compensate the Eastbourne fishermen for lost tackle and damaged boats.

The coming of the railway on 14 May 1849 was the beginning of Eastbourne as we know it. The line had reached Brighton in 1841, Lewes in 1846, and Polegate by 1849, from where Eastbourne passengers had to complete their journey by horse omnibus, horseback or, not unusually, on foot. The original intention was for the railway to run through Willingdon village and terminate at Old Town, but the line further east only required a cutting in the final approach. The station was in about the middle of today's Terminus Road, in front of the post office, where a wooden hut along Wharf Road awaited the wonder of the age. On the big day a 'large party' sat down to a cold collation prepared by the landlord of the *Gilbert Arms* and served in a booth erected near today's Central Library. Mr Freeman Thomas

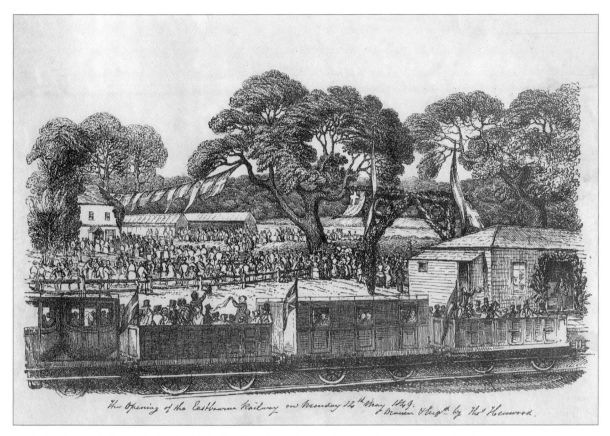

20 Eastbourne's first train in 1849. The building in the left background is the Hartfield farmhouse, converted to the *Gilbert Arms*, and right foreground is the tiny wooden station. The tremendous revelry lasted from sunrise to midnight for many residents had never seen a steam locomotive. Near midday this special train puffed in bearing officials of the London Brighton and South Coast Railway Company, who were greeted by the great and good of Eastbourne accompanied by a brass band playing 'Behold the conquering hero comes'.

of Ratton presided, there were the usual toasts, and the rest of the day was spent on celebrations, winding up with a grand firework display.

Until 1868 the town wasn't directly connected to the outside world. A local train met the Hastings train at Polegate station and, on a single track until 1862, shuttled to and from Eastbourne. Even so, the railway had an enormous impact on the town. In 1851 John Davies Gilbert constructed Terminus Road over farmland from the station to Seaside Road, linking up with Victoria Place (now part of Terminus Road) to give access to the seafront. Built for residential villas, it became the main shopping centre so needed widening in 1894 and 1898, but it was never the grand boulevard the town required.

The railway also meant that the wholesale movement of quality goods and heavy materials was possible with less reliance on locally available wares. It drove most stage-coaches out of business, the roads were emptied of long-distance traffic, and the coaching inns subsided into local pubs until they were resuscitated by the motor car in the 1930s.[18] Railway mania resulted in many madcap schemes, including that for a Newhaven and Eastbourne line through tunnels under the Downs to Friston, then across the Cuckmere Valley, and with another cutting to Seaford.[19] The Davies Gilberts had a mind to create a seaside resort at Birling Gap, with a direct line from Polegate, but the motor car put an end to that.

21 Hartfield Farm, at the junction of the present Terminus Road and Grove Road, was converted into an inn, the *Gilbert Arms*. The signboard bore the crest of the Gilbert family, which included a squirrel, giving rise to the name favoured by all Eastbourne, *The Squirrel*. The farmer, John Pennington Gorringe, was moved to Upperton Farm by the Davies Gilberts, who owned both properties.

The 1851 census showed that the population of 3,433 had only increased by 400 in ten years, with scant incoming, for almost all the households were born and bred in Sussex, apart from the few professionals and the coastguards who had always been rotated around the stations to avoid any possibility of collusion.

The first reference to Eastbourne in law was in 1803.[20] Apart from the lords of the manor there were no local magistrates before 1852; the town was policed by the county force, and until 1842 there was only one county policeman in the area – and he was stationed at Pevensey. Traditions hallowed by time survived. The stocks in Grove Road were used for drunks who could not pay their fine into the 1850s, and as a part of the division of the Crumbles in 1851 the lordship of the manor of Eastbourne fell to the Davies Gilberts.

The world was being convulsed by new ideas and new processes, however. An important catalyst, Charles Robert Darwin, wrote part of *The Origin*

of Species while on holiday in 1850 at Seahouses, in what is now Marine Parade. The coming of the railway meant former hamlets were poised to become an elegant and prestigious resort for the wealthy middle classes, guided by the patronage of the landowners and by the residents' pride in their town, as well as the investment of businessmen. Eastbourne was fortunate in that the two families who owned the land, the Cavendishes and the Davies Gilberts, had vision and were well served by their agents and trustees. It is thanks to their sage measures that Eastbourne owes much of its charm.

When the Royal Princes were here, and up to 1850, the land around the town remained divided into strips, relics of medieval times. Farmers tended to farm a number of adjacent strips by agreement, but separate ownership hampered expansion. In 1840 the Cavendishes and the Davies Gilberts enclosed the land so that it could be developed and, after settling with the church, which claimed its share, by 1851 Eastbourne was ripe for development.

Two

Before the Royal Princes

Like most seaside towns before the discovery of the virtues and vices of sea bathing, Eastbourne was a hamlet of farmers and a few fishermen, although people had been eking out a living here for thousands of years.[1] The axes of Stone Age man have been found at Beachy Head, but the first signs of agriculture, discernible here about 6,000 years ago, were a major cultural change. For the first time people stayed in one place and needed to protect a choice site from marauders with bank and ditch clearances. Fields and stones therefore marked these communities, tool-making skills improved, wheat, oats and barley were cultivated and animals domesticated. Neolithic axes have been found in Kings Drive, and a scraper was found at Bullock Down, on Beachy Head.

There is little evidence in Sussex for the early Bronze Age when, at last, metal tools were made and a start was made on clearing the Wealden forest for farming. The era is associated with a line of burial mounds, bowl barrows, running five miles from Beachy Head to Willingdon Hill.[2] In 1805 gold bracelets were found on the beach near the Wish Tower, and a barbed arrowhead and Mortlake-style pottery have been found at Bullock Down, along with a collared rim food vessel and two crouched burial and cremation sites. Working iron demanded higher temperatures, but the harder tools created meant it was easier to clear forests for cattle, and the heavier plough enabled a greater variety of soils to be cultivated. As a result 'Celtic fields', or Iron-Age field banks, are found scattered over the neighbouring Downland. These were not intentional, but built up when cultivating a hillside, and perpetuate the small, square outline of the original fields. As agriculture improved people were better fed and the population increased. Four

bracelets have been found at Heathy Brow, on Beachy Head, which was an Iron-Age settlement with mixed farming, mainly sheep.

The Romans, under Claudius, invaded Britain in A.D. 43, with no opposition in Sussex. The Eastbourne area had been under the Regni tribe, and their King, Cogidubnus, was in contact with the Romans and welcomed them; Tacitus mentions him as faithful to the Romans. They brought dramatic change, offering peace, law, security, civilisation, trade and new religions, and introducing the first decent roads, concrete, bricks, tiles, nails, locks, piped hot water, and unguents. Within two generations they had established towns, imported exotic goods, brought prosperity and introduced the idea of a nation.

The locals adopted Roman habits and customs, as well as their temples, baths and centrally-heated country villas with the latest feature, straight walls and right-angled corners. The use of coins for monetary purposes spread rapidly, the staters previously having been used only for display. Inscribed Roman stonework is rare in southern England, but blue and red decoration implying a wealthy family is known.

Near the Wish Tower a port developed, Longus Portus. Greensand was quarried beside today's *Cavendish Hotel*, and just to the east of the pier an elaborate, opulent, mainly first-century villa dominated the area, with three or four tenant farms around.[3] The Roman economy was based on farming, in the Eastbourne area a corn-sheep system, to support the sophisticated lifestyle of the towns, and to provision the army.[4] The Romans had more land under cultivation around Eastbourne than in the Second World War, and the corn surplus went to the Classis Britannica, the Roman transport and

22 Beachy Head. Eastbourne lies at the meeting of the Wealden clay and the chalky South Downs. Beachy Head took 15-20 million years to form, and the area was subsequently lifted up to create the Downs. The Normans gave the headland the name *Beau Chef*.

23 The most spectacular discovery at Eastbourne's Bronze-Age Shinewater settlement was a 3,000-year-old bronze sickle with a bird's-eye field-maple handle. In August 1995 Lawrence Stevens observed ancient timbers protruding from an area of black peat east of the town, and identified the site as a Bronze-Age settlement. (Photograph N. Taylor)

24 David Galer, the Towner Gallery curator, pointing out a man-made shaft in the cliff near Belle Tout exposed by erosion of the chalk in 1971. Some suggested that it might be a well but the date is uncertain: Belle Tout was favoured with a Stone-Age site, a Bronze-Age site and a late Iron-Age hillfort. The Beaker people, of 4,000 years ago, named after their distinctive pottery, also had one of their few sites in south-east England around the hillock.

supply fleet, and later the Roman naval base at Pevensey.

The existence of a Roman villa in Eastbourne was verified in 1712. The remains were left exposed and by 1743 the Rev. Jeremiah Milles wrote, 'a great part of the Roman bath and mosaic pavement has been washed away'.[5] When the Round House was demolished in 1841 more pavement was found, and Roman coins and pottery have turned up all over the town. On Bullock Down two native peasant settlements have yielded quite exotic objects, from finger rings to a brooch with enamel inlay.[6]

Saxon pirates from Germany began raiding the southern coasts in their shallow-draught longboats, and after A.D. 300 the Romano-British fleet could not contain them. The Emperor Diocletian created the position of Count of the Saxon Shore to curb these raids, and naval bases were built at vulnerable estuaries, from the Isle of Wight to the Wash, linked by watch towers and signal stations. Each base had a massive stone fortress, and Anderitum at Pevensey was the last to be built, in about 335. It was of an unusual oval shape to conform to the confines of the peninsular site which provided a natural harbour and protection against the prevailing winds. At this

25 An Iron-Age Hallstatt 'onion' urn of 2,500 years ago dug up in Green Street, Old Town in 1921. It had collapsed in the firing and the 'waster' been buried. Although the potter's wheel came into Britain before the Romans, hand-made pottery continued in Sussex.

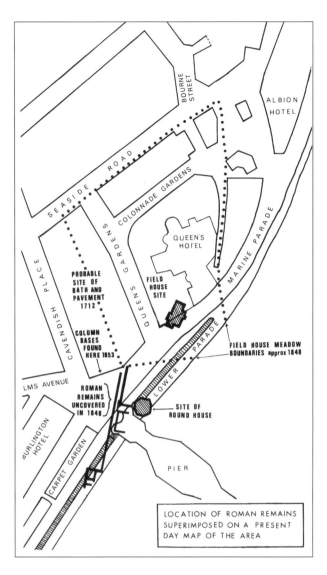

LOCATION OF ROMAN REMAINS
SUPERIMPOSED ON A PRESENT
DAY MAP OF THE AREA

26 Plan of Eastbourne's Roman villa. In 1712 Thomas Willard's field by the seashore was found to contain 'pavement edged with bricks … and tessera, exactly straight and well cemented'. In 1841 and 1848 Roman foundations were exposed during the building of the sea wall. In 1853, when Grand Parade was being built, the bases of two columns were found. 'They were left for some days for the inspection of the curious and then broken up and built into the foundations.'

27 Roman single box-flue tile. First-century pottery shards have been found in Ringwood Road; roof tiles, spindle whorls and pottery in Arundel Road; a salt extraction site in Prideaux Road; and a spearhead and coins at Bullock Down. Samples of flue tiles, a portion of pavement and an amphora handle found at Eastbourne are in the Towner Museum. Cremation urns and coins help date the finds.

time an inlet stretched to Polegate, with tiny islands known as 'Eyes', a general name persisting in Hydneye, Winkney and Anten's Eye – now St Anthony's Hill.

The Romans left about 410, and in 477 the Saxon Aelle landed near Chichester but met resistance at Eastbourne, probably from local militia. The Saxons returned some years later and in 491 they stormed Pevensey Castle, about the last place to hold out; according to the *Anglo-Saxon Chronicle* 'not one Briton was left alive'.

The transition to Anglo-Saxon society was not as violent or as destructive of Romano-British culture as biased accounts would have us believe, but all Celtic names were obliterated. Some Saxons even landed by agreement and the Britons (Celts) were amalgamated, perhaps as slaves. The Saxons settled down and by the sixth century Sussex was a South-Saxon kingdom. Although most Britons had been Christian in Roman times, many had lapsed or reverted to paganism, and Sussex was about the last county to be re-converted, in about 680, by St Wilfrid.

The next wave of boat-invaders, the Danes, appeared in 790. They posed a serious threat until the efforts of King Alfred the Great gave the country

28 Coin of Postumus (258-68) found on Bullock Down. Over 17,000 coins were found on the Downs between 1879 and 1973, with dates of Hadrian (117-38), Faustima I (*c.*140), Antoninus Pius (138-61) and other coins of 330-5. The main find of 5,294 coins was by local farmer Eddie Williams in 1961; they were probably buried because they had been superseded – and they are of no value today either. The 1973 hoard was buried in a Henmoor-type bronze bucket, only the second found in Britain.

29 Iron spearhead found in a male grave, and sixth-century brooches usually found in female graves (not to scale), from the old Eastbourne College of Arts & Technology site in 1997. Saxons left few records but a succession of burial sites stretching from St Anne's Road to Willingdon Road confirms a long occupation.

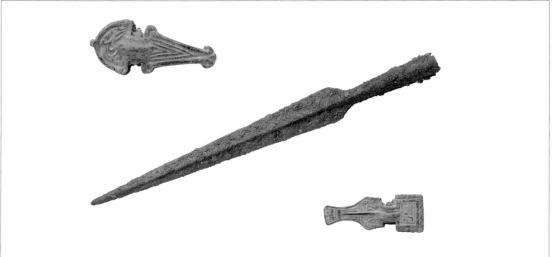

a century of peace. Eastbourne even became part of the royal estate. The first mention we have of Bourne is in 963, and various theories exist as to why 'East' was added.[7] Was it to differentiate it from a (West)bourne, or did it derive from Easthall, an ancient name for the Old Town area, or from 'est', the Celtic for 'water'?

The Danes returned in 980 and some stayed, King Canute ruling over much of southern England. Yet by 1054, Edward the Confessor's time, there is a record of a wooden church in Eastbourne, although like most Saxon churches no trace remains. The penultimate invaders of Britain were the Norwegians, who were soundly defeated by King Harold; but at same time William of Normandy landed between Eastbourne and Hastings, probably at Bulverhythe, although Norman's Bay, nearer Eastbourne, has a claim. After Harold's defeat by William, now the Conqueror, Eastbourne was handed to Robert, Count of Mortain, William's half-brother.

The Norman conquest meant another upheaval, and any opposition was dealt with severely. The barons put up imposing castles to control their new-won lands; some were wooden initially, but all were soon immense stone structures exuding power. Robert of Mortain built one within the perimeter

30 Motcombe pond with Motcombe farmhouse behind and, to the left, Motcombe Baths, opened in 1905. The Bourne flowed from a chalk spring strong enough to drive a watermill in The Goffs, then ran along Southfields Road to form a sheepwash near the Central Library. It continued by Terminus Road to between Tideswell and Langney Roads until at Seaside it formed a pond, the Broadbourne, which seeped through the shingle into the sea. Now enclosed, it can be seen from the footpath between 46 and 48 The Goffs when in spate. It supplied Eastbourne with both its name and with drinkable water.

of the Roman fortress at Pevensey. In Domesday Book of 1086 the Bourne Hundred had a church, a watermill and saltpans:

> In Eastbourne Hundred the Count of Mortain holds Borne in Lordship. King Edward [the Confessor] held it. There were and are 46 hides. Land for 28 ploughs. In Lordship 4 ploughs, 68 villagers and 3 smallholders with 28 ploughs. 1 mill at 5s.; 16 salts at £4 40d.; meadow 25 acres; from pasture £6. ... Roger the cleric ... Walter holds Easthall from the Count ... value before 1066 50s.; later 30s.; now 40s.[8]

This suggests a population of some 350, the financial impact of 1066 and a recovery. A 'hide' was a land measurement, while a 'Hundred' was the Saxon division of a county. The Eastbourne Hundred was sub-divided into Upperton, Easthall, Lamport,

Meads and Upwick. The county was split by the Normans into six Rapes, Eastbourne being in Pevensey Rape.

The Normans replaced wooden churches with stone buildings and in 1160 the church at the Bourne crossroads was started. The stimulus was the appointment in 1150 of the Treasurer of Chichester Cathedral as Rector of Eastbourne. The Caen stone would be shipped over in boats that were run up the beaches to discharge in the same fashion as the colliers many years later.

The town remained an isolated farming community, with a little fishing, for the next few hundred years and agriculture remained the prime occupation until the 1800s. Eastbourne is fortunately situated: to the west lie high chalk grasslands, ideal for sheep, for they need less water than cattle and

31 The Jesus House in Church Street was demolished in 1895; the site is now St Mary's Court. It was owned by one of the six guilds in Eastbourne which were suppressed by 1550 along with St Gregory's Chapel. Afterwards they operated as friendly societies until wound up. When in 1540 Henry VIII divorced Anne of Cleves, part of the provision he made for her was a portion of the tithes on lands in Eastbourne.

enjoy the short Downland turf, while the lower slopes of the Downs have rich arable land with plenty of water. The scarp runs from Meads to Willingdon, and the droveways, such as Pashley or Willingdon Drove, were ancient paths used to drive beasts from the Downs to the levels. These lush marshes, formed behind Le Crumble shingle bar, were perfect cattle fattening meadows in the summer, and were being drained. Their maintenance was the responsibility of the Commissioners of the Levels from the Middle Ages.

The Count of Mortain lost the Manor of Bourne when he backed the wrong side in a royal succession. The manor passed through at least 19 more pairs of hands before, in 1308, Edward II gave it to Bartholomew de Badlesmere. He probably never lived at Eastbourne, but he extended Eastbourne's

parish church, and was granted charters for a weekly market and yearly fair. He became the Constable of three castles, and a Steward of the Royal Household, but sided against Edward II and his favourites. Taken prisoner at the Battle of Boroughbridge, he was hanged as a rebel and his estates went to the Crown. With the accession of Edward III, Badlesmere's widow, Margaret, was restored to the estates in 1330. The Manors of Bourne and Eckington descended to a daughter, Margery, who had married William, Lord de Roos, whose family held Bourne in an almost continuous line until 1555.

Badlesmere's fair developed into a sheep fair, with the sheep held on Summerdown. The rector of Eastbourne was granted a charter in 1232 to hold a three-day fair at Michaelmas, and this continued for 670 years. It was held in the churchyard at first, but

32 White flints in St Leonard's Place. Examples of chequered flints (mixed with brick or stone) are seen in the parish church of St Mary, while Christ Church, Seaside, St Michael's and All Angels at Ocklynge, and St John's in Meads all have white flints (mined flints). Holy Trinity has white flints in the nave, and cobbles or kidney flints (rounded off by the sea) in the tower. There are many secular samples, mainly in Old Town. Flint Halls in Church Street has white flints in black mortar in the front wall. Flint walls abound.

when this practice was banned in 1285 the booths and stalls were set out on the surrounding roads. In the absence of shops it was almost the only opportunity to buy goods, and an excuse for merchants and farmers to frequent the *Lamb Inn*.

In 1348-9 a new, and more feared, invader ravished Britain. Sussex suffered badly from the Black Death, or Plague, and it was an initial cause of many villages being deserted, including Excete on Cuckmere Haven, although French raids didn't help. With the death of perhaps a third of the population, the scarcity of labour led to immense social change and threatened the end of the medieval system of serfs working strips of land under control

of the local lord of the manor. These changes were slow to reach Sussex, but arable farming tended to give way to pasture after 1400, being less labour intensive, and the village was soon a major sheep-farming centre with, reputedly, over 4,000 animals.

The final dissolution of the monasteries was a time of high inflation, and social climbers did well if they could keep their heads. In 1554/5 the Earl of Rutland, a descendant of the de Roos family, sold off the Great Manor of Bourne to three such climbers of Eastbourne. The Burton family bought some 280 acres, taking as their manor house Bourne Place (now the front of Compton Place). The Rev. Dr William Burton sold the estate to a stepson,

33 Compton Place Lodge, with an inset of knapped and squared flints. Top-drawer flints were knapped (split to show a smooth, dark surface) and squared (flaked to form a rectangle). This work took time and skill and so these expensive flints are found at Compton Place, Compton Place Lodge, and the Belvedere on Paradise Links.

William Wilson, in 1644, and in turn the Wilson family sold to Spencer Compton, Earl of Wilmington, whence it came to the Dukes of Devonshire by marriage. Another part was acquired by Thomas Gildredge, who had his manor house in what is now The Goffs. In 1668 this manor passed in the female line to the Gilbert family. John Selwyn, who lived at Friston Place, took the north-west part. His grand-daughter married a Parker and the Ratton lands were merged with her dowry as Eastbourne-Parker manor.

Eastbourne might have had a beacon near Beachy Head, but otherwise wasn't well prepared for the Armada; the 1587 Survey found 'two 40-year-old Sakers and three Robinets unfurnished with powder and shot'.[9] Fortunately the Elizabethan privateers, and the English weather were the victors, which gave rise to the British age of exploration, including more travel around Britain. In 1580 William Camden journeyed eastwards 'to Cuckmer, a very considerable harbour. Crossing over the promontory called beach we come to Pevensey.'[10] If Camden thought a place wasn't worth commenting upon, he didn't. Such was Eastbourne's fate.

It does seem that Eastbourne suffered a period of decay in the late 1500s. John Norden in 1594 noticed the place, but observed that it was 'a poore market Towne ... the fishermen spend what they get … which decayeth the Towne'. Parish records name three fishermen drowned in 1605. Fishing families date back to 1296, when Erridge was a name on the list of taxpayers. The name continues in the town, and at the November 1902 rescue of SS *Southport* no fewer than eight Erridges were members of the lifeboat crew. Another fishing family, the Hides, can trace their ancestors back to the 1500s. None are now in fishing.

Eastbourne's worst year for the plague, with 108 deaths, was 1616 when the population was perhaps 800. The poorly constructed houses, allowing easy access for rats, facilitated the spread of plague, and the introduction of chimneys in the late 1500s and the increased use of bricks and flints for houses during the 1600s helped bring an end to these regular epidemics. Flint from the Downs is very hard and durable silica; it was used for roads and local buildings because it was cheap and widely available, but it has limitations because it comes in small pieces and is difficult to dress.[11]

The Civil War passed Eastbourne by but caused many heartaches and tragedies among its gentry such as the Parker family of Ratton. Sir Thomas Parker was a Parliamentarian and his younger brother Henry became secretary to Oliver Cromwell. On the other hand, his son-in-law, Sir William Campion, married to Grace Parker with a son born in 1640, was a Royalist who defended Boarstall House against Fairfax but was killed in a skirmish in 1649.

34   The 800-ton *Nympha Americana*, which broke up as it ran ashore near Birling Gap on 29 November 1747, was perhaps the most sensational of the Beachy Head shipwrecks because of its rich cargo, £30,000 of quicksilver, and £5,000 in silver and gold coins. While Eastbourne folk don't appear to have gone in for ship wrecking, they did consider that a wreck on their patch was fair game. One Exciseman, Thomas Fletcher, commended for his work in recovering cargo, was killed by smugglers in 1750. His grave is in Friston churchyard.

William, the 3rd Earl of Devonshire, kept his estates intact during the Civil War and Commonwealth by living in obscurity in France. The Wilsons were Royalists. An oft-told story relates how a detachment of Parliamentarian dragoons came to search Bourne Place in 1658 and William Wilson set before them a meal of wheatear pie, considered a great delicacy, thereby providing the household with time to destroy evidence of their Royalist associations.[12]

John Boulte, minister of Eastbourne during the Commonwealth, had 29 children by two wives, but found time to keep careful parish registers with full details, something which few ministers managed. The entries for 1651 reveal some village tragedies. 'Thomas Buckle, a poor man, died of starvation.' Richard Marden was 'slain by a fall at a chalk pit'. William Bartholomew, 'near 6-years-old', was drowned in the sheepwash. John Basher was most unfortunate to be 'killed from the overthrowing of a dung cart' and sadly, 'a bastard man-child, unbaptised' of Alice Basset was drowned by his mother in the millpond.

With the advent of the Bank of England, burgeoning joint-stock companies and the Act of Union, the country was beginning to acquire overseas possessions. The 1690 Battle of Beachy Head fought three leagues south of the headland, where the light tower is today, would have been clearly visible from the cliffs. As usual, the British and French were involved, but in view of the 'inconclusive' result no further reference will be made.[13] Budgen states that a Captain Francis Scarlett, who had an estate in Jamaica, was a native of Eastbourne, and from 1623 the Freeman Thomas family of Ratton had owned land in the West Indies.[14] The middle classes were moving into land. In 1697 The Lawns estate in Old Town was bought by Thomas Willard. By the early 1800s, after three generations, John and Nicholas Willard lived respectively at The Lawns and The Greys. A Tudor house, from 1588, The Greys was the residence of the vicars of Eastbourne. Both estates now have roads named after them.[15]

To the mariner of the time Beachy Head was fearsome, and hundreds of ships have been wrecked off the headland. The earliest name we have is the *Marie* of Santander in 1368, but most went unrecorded, or appeared in the parish registers under 'burial of seaman washed ashore'. There was also harrying of ships, and Eastbourne folk lined up along the Beachy Head cliff in 1778 to watch the *Greyhound* see off a French cutter attempting to capture colliers. Whatever the dangers, the 1700s saw a further upsurge in travel, as the nobility with time and money to spare took advantage of the opportunities. Visits to Eastbourne were encouraged because the Downs of Sussex, 'the finest Carpet in the World', made for easy riding. In 1713 Macky wrote, 'I lay at a pretty village called Eastborn and supped upon some little birds called Whit-ears. This village lies under the promontory so famous for the Loss of Ships, called Beachy Head.'[16]

The Wilson family did not live at Bourne Place after 1718, when Spencer Compton MP became the tenant.[17] Elizabeth Spencer, only daughter of a rich cloth merchant, had eloped with his great-grandfather, William Compton, 1st Earl of Northampton, in the 16th century, and Spencer Compton was already owner of Sussex properties from his stepmother, Lady Isabel Sackville. In 1724 he bought the Bourne Place estate from the Wilsons, and had the house, now Compton Place, remodelled and enlarged by Colen Campbell between 1726 and 1731. With Spencer Compton, a politician of national standing, in residence, more of his class were attracted to Eastbourne, just as the nascent practice of sea bathing was spreading. In 1738 the Earl and Countess of Oxford, their family and attendants 'stayed at Mr. Thomas Smith's *Lamb* at East Bourn'. Their son's tutor, George Vertue, wrote, 'The Earl of Wilmington has a seat here. He came to visit Earl and Lady Oxford.'

In 1754 the Rev. Dr Richard Pococke wrote, 'I went to the seahouses near East Bourne, very pleasantly situated on the beach and the people resort here to bathe and drink the sea water. I went to East Bourne where the Earl of Northampton has a seat. The sea cliffs here are high and very fine springs of water run out of them.'[18] So Eastbourne was getting known. Edward, Baron Thurlow, the Solicitor General and Attorney

35 A ceiling at Compton Place. John Whaley visited about 1735: 'We rode along the Sands to East Bourne. In the parish is the seat of Spencer Compton, Earl of Wilmington ... The house is partly new cased of the Outside and the Inside is entirely new, in fitting up which a vast deal of money thrown away. All agreed that the ceilings were very fine.' [ESPRO AMS 5937 10 & 13/81735]

General in the 1770s, lived for a while in the town, which was producing its own sons of note. John Hamilton Mortimer ARA, born in the High Street in 1740, misspent a wild youth painting legendary scenes, and Edward Daniel Clarke, born at Willingdon in 1769, was the first Professor of Mineralogy at Cambridge. Said to have invented the oxy-hydrogen blowlamp, he also published his *Travels*, to Scotland, Italy, Finland and Siberia, in six volumes.

Sam Beckett, innkeeper of the '*Angel*, Sea Side', advertised in 1761 that he had a good four-wheel post-chaise with a careful driver; as this driver once managed to pierce a horse he was overtaking with the shaft of the chaise, heaven knows what he got up to in his careless moments! Seahouses also had a *Ship Inn* in the 1760s so the few people there were well provided. Cooper's brewery started as Chapman's in about 1749, and William Hurst founded the Old Town Brewery in 1777. The Hursts were a family of bakers, brewers, publicans and millers who were established in Old Town by 1764.

William Hickey, who with three companions was ferried ashore to Seahouses after a stormy channel trip in 1776, commented, 'The boatman conducted us to a miserable looking dwelling where we expected neither victuals, nor drink'. Inside,

36 A seizure at the Eastbourne Customs House in the 18th century. Barrels are being unloaded from a cart labelled 'Birling'. In the 1700s and early 1800s large quantities of brandy, gin, tobacco, tea and, following a 1766 embargo, lace were landed in this area. The fisher folk were involved but it must have been worthwhile, for if a fisherman were found guilty his boat was sawn in two. According to Richard Gilbert, there was a dry well on the beach, opposite Howard Square, in which smugglers stored their ankers or barrels.

however, 'The landlady had a blazing fire going in a clean room, and half an hour afterwards we sat down to as fine a dish of fish as ever seen at Billingsgate, with excellent lobster and oyster sauces, followed by a pair of well-dressed chickens washed down with ale, and finished with cheese. A casual enquiry revealed that the landlady did have some wine "which might not be good enough for gentlemen of quality"; nevertheless a bottle was called for and pronounced, "…as high-flavoured a claret as any in my own cellar", and each of us drank two bottles.

'The bill came to six shillings; "And what are we to pay for the drink?" "Oh I make no charge for that. Now and then, my boys run over to Guernsey on business and bring home a few dozen bottles, so as it costs me nothing you are heartily welcome." We ascertained that her boys were smugglers and with considerable difficulty prevailed upon her to accept a guinea for as excellent a repast as four hungry fellows had ever sat down to.'[19]

Coastal trading had taken place from Eastbourne beach for hundreds of years and smuggling had become a way of life – and death, a Riding officer was killed at Langney in 1717. A Customs House was situated at Seahouses, to the west of the present Ordnance Yard, and Excise officials (a separate

37 The nearest of Eastbourne's many windmills is Gildredge Manor postmill (or Black Mill) in St Anne's Road, demolished in 1878; next is Rectory Mill (or White or Parsonage Mill) near Watts Lane; behind is St John's Mill (Hurst's or Upperton Mill) in Mill Road, and in the distance is Ocklynge Mill. St John's was a tower mill (only the cap rotates to catch the wind) next to Ocklynge Manor House, which was finally demolished for flats in 1986, although a millstone has been incorporated into the boundary wall.

service) operated alongside the Customs men from the 17th century, probably using the warehouse known to have stood in Church Street on the site of Edgmond Hall.[20] There are a few records of Eastbourne's complicity in these illicit proceedings. The *Gentleman's Magazine* of 13 June 1774 reports, 'The officers of the customs at Eastbourne, having intelligence of smugglers, went with five Dragoons to the seashore, but 100 smugglers rode up, fired shots at the customs officers, and disarmed them before loading the goods on above 100 horses.' An Eastbourne letter of 2 March 1784 states, 'Yesterday evening two cutters from the continent landed their cargoes a short distance from this place, a great part of which was conveyed away by men with horses, but tea was left behind to the amount of £200.'[21]

Most of Britain's tobacco was smuggled, and Crowlink to the west was the conduit of so much smuggled gin that a 'Crowlink Geneva' was peddled around London. Smuggling, however, wasn't the romantic escapade so often portrayed; threatened with hanging or transportation if caught, the smugglers were ruthless ruffians with little regard for life and property.

Eastbourne was well provided with windmills, of which 17 are known near the town; Ocklynge Hill and St Anne's Hill had four each, and Pashley Down two.[22] In addition there were two watermills on the Bourne Stream, three horizontal mills, and a tide mill at Langney. None are left in Eastbourne, but Old Town still has some quaint and ancient buildings, including one of the finest churches in the diocese, a 13/14th-century guild house, a medieval dovecote, one of the oldest inns in the county, and the nearby Pillory Green. Viewed from the west the interior of the parish church of St Mary the Virgin is of great beauty. Unusually, the chancel floor is a step below the level of the nave. The oak screens dating from the 14th century are the finest Decorated examples in Sussex, and the oldest brass is a small tablet commemorating 'John Kyng Rector d.1445 Treasurer of the Church of Chichester and proprietor of this Church'.

38 St Mary's Church *c.*1800. Built in the Norman style, this replaced a Saxon church dedicated to St Michael, which was probably nearer Ocklynge. In the 14th century the nave was extended and the tower added. It is a mixture of Caen stone, flint and Eastbourne greensand. An extensive restoration was undertaken in the mid-19th century, when the roofs were re-covered and the tower repaired. Adjoining the church to the right is the Old Parsonage, a good specimen of a 15/16th-century Rectory Manor farmhouse.

... Sacred to the Memory of Henry Lushington ...

... At ye age of sixteen in 1754 he embarqued for Bengal in ye service of ye India Company and attaining a perfect knowledge of ye Persian language made himself essentially useful. It is difficult to determine whether he excelled more in a civil or a military capacity. His activity in both recommended him to the notice and esteem of Lord Clive; whom with equal credit to himself and to his patron he served in the different characters of Secretary, Interpreter and Commissary. In ye year of 1756, by a melancholy revolution, he was with others to ye amount of 146 forced into a dungeon at Calcutta so small that 23 only escaped. He was one of the survivors, but reserved for greater misery, for by a subsequent revolution in the year 1763, he was with 200 more taken prisoner at Patna, and after a tedious confinement being singled out with John Ellis and William Hay Esq. was by order of the Nabob Cossim Ally Kawn and under the direction of one Someroo, an apostate European, deliberately and inhumanely murdered ...

39 Near the west end of the south wall of St Mary's Church is this inscription to Henry Lushington, son of the Rev. Dr Henry Lushington, Vicar of Eastbourne 1734-79. Having survived the Black Hole of Calcutta, he was killed seven years later. When the first man was butchered he seized a scimitar from one of his assailants and killed three and wounded two of the attackers, 'until at length oppressed with numbers he greatly fell'. 'May the rising generation admire and imitate such an example.'

40 Pilgrims in Borough Lane, which started as a resting house for pilgrims, owned by a religious guild. It is a Wealden house, to which is attached a one-up, one-down cottage. The hall reaches to the ceiling except at each end where there are upstairs solars. The many interesting features include 14th-century jettying, a chimney and queen post of 16th-century construction, a bay window of 1784, and proving ovens for yeast near the inglenook. There are no foundations; the cellars in solid chalk date from about 1130.

The church contains almost 100 memorials to Eastbourne notables, including representatives of the Brodie, Cavendish, Gilbert, Marchant, Mortimer, Pitman, Tollemache, Ventris and Willard families, and one to Hart, the verger from 1914 to 42, who was the last of an unbroken line of vergers over 202 years. The north wall of the Gildredge chapel has a memorial to Katherine Gildredge, who died in 1629, sculptured by Edward Marshall, who in 1660 was appointed mason to the Crown. One can only assume this was an early piece and thus affordable by a provincial landowner. The east window of St Michael replaces a medieval one, destroyed by bombing in 1943, which had six pieces of 16th-century Flemish glass. The Rev. Walter Budgen made a record of monumental inscriptions in 1900, which is at Lewes.[23]

There would have been a ring of bells from the time the tower was built. With the introduction of change ringing the need was for more easily handled bells and in 1650 they were melted down and recast. In 1714 £8 was paid for re-hanging a bell which broke its axle on full swing, fell two floors, missed the ringer by a fraction, struck the arch of the tower, and sank a foot into the pavement without cracking.

The oldest secular building in the town is probably Pilgrims in Borough Lane. The house opposite was built by the Rev. Dr Henry Lushington over 1776/7, shortly before his second

41   The house built by the Rev. Dr Henry Lushington *c.*1776, and sold by his son Stephen in 1792 to Charles Gilbert, who moved his household there from the Manor House in The Goffs five years later. The Gilberts had been building up their land holdings in the area, resulting in Eastbourne being effectively divided between themselves and the Cavendishes. This is currently the Towner Art Gallery and Local Museum.

marriage, and in 1797 it became the Gildredge-Gilbert Manor House. The *Lamb Inn* was where public proclamations were delivered, and where the Fifth of November bonfires were held.[24] Both the *Star* and the *Lamb* were probably resting places for mendicant friars and pilgrims. We know William Bartholomew was landlord in 1606, and in 1761 the *Lamb* was advertised as 'a good accustomed Inn with proper stables thereto'. With the *New Inn* it was also a starting point for the London coach.

William Hickey wrote, 'Eastbourne, only insignificant ... scattered houses in August 1776, since become a fashionable place of resort'. But with royal patronage and the railway, his 'miserable-looking' seafront was to experience a transformation.

42   The *Lamb Inn*'s 16th-century timbers are above an Early English cellar which has a central roof boss of a style common in the 14th century. In 1635 a Lieutenant Hammond wrote, 'rid all along by the Sands to the holy quiet *Lamb* in Borne'. In 1912 a runaway horse damaged the front re-exposing the timbers so most of the Georgian plaster (seen here) was stripped away. Stories of underground passages are probably just that; there is no evidence for their existence.

Three

Increased Prospects 1850-1900

William, the 2nd Earl of Burlington, noted in his diary that the coming of the railway to the sleepy village of Eastbourne 'certainly increased the prospects of the place considerably'. He did his bit, too, for in the next five years he invested £37,000 in constructing Eastbourne's first sea wall and villas to entice the wealthy to the town. James Berry, county surveyor and architect to the Earl, set out a plan for the town in 1847. The first part, Grand Parade, was commenced in the spring of 1851, and the foundation stone could be seen in a corner of number 5. Builders took up the plots, and Victoria Place (the sea end of Terminus Road) and Cavendish Place were started. Tenants, however, were thin on the ground and all the builders went bankrupt. Even

worse, when the Earl endeavoured to dispose of their efforts at auction there were no takers.

The original Marine Parade commenced just by the *Albion Hotel* and ended at the Round House, near today's pier. It was barely above the beach, and the 2m. wide, slab-covered stretch was constantly washed by the sea. Berry built his new Marine Parade sea wall from Field House (near the *Queens Hotel*) to Victoria Place, using blocks of greensand found on the spot. He laid them end-on to the sea and set each tier back a foot, to break the force of the waves, but the greensand was not hard enough to bear the pounding.

Berry also tackled Eastbourne's water supply. Most of Motcombe Gardens was a lake, so in 1857 he

43   Grand Parade as envisaged in 1851. It was the 7th Duke of Devonshire-to-be who saw the potential of the sea, the beach and the magnificent Beachy Head. The famous flower beds in front of the Parade, the Carpet Gardens, date to the 1850s. They were owned and maintained by the *Burlington Hotel* at 14 Grand Parade until sold to the Town Council. The name derives from the oriental carpet patterns on which they were modelled.

44 Devonshire Place *c.*1873, and the seated bronze of William, 7th Duke of Devonshire (1808-91) at the sea end of his glorious avenue today. When the unmarried 6th Duke (1790-1858) died, a cousin's son, our 2nd Earl of Burlington, became the 7th Duke and brought the Eastbourne estates, including Compton Place, into the dukedom. Eastbournians showed their appreciation of his 'worthy life' by erecting this Goscombe John statue in 1901.

cleared the spring and created the present square pond as a reservoir, from which water was distributed. Eastbourne's increasing population required more radical measures, though, so the new Duke of Devonshire decided to rid himself of Berry. Following the 1859 Eastbourne Waterworks Act he formed the Eastbourne Waterworks Company, 'for better supplying with water the Town of Eastbourne and places adjacent'. George Ambrose Wallis was

engineer to the water company. He cleared out the Bedford well in 1859 and erected a pumping station with wells and headings at Waterworks Road, and this supply coped until the 1890s.

Henry Currey, a family member of the Devonshire's legal advisers, was appointed the Duke's agent at Eastbourne. In 1859 he produced a comprehensive plan for the Duke's estate, including Meads, which with the Duke's money

45 Cornfield Terrace, built by John Gosden, fitted on a medieval farm strip and was one of the few developments not on Cavendish or Gilbert land. Farmer Gosden had 1,180 acres in 1861, employing 39 men and 11 boys. Samuel Bradford, the coal merchant, once had to ask Gosden for payment and was told to call for it at his home the next day before four o'clock. Bradford was there at 3a.m. and had to throw gravel at Gosden's windows to wake him up. Henceforth the two regularly settled up at that time.

and support would see the best designed seaside resort in England. Currey also contrived St Thomas' Hospital, London. Outsiders began to move in. Edward Maynard erected houses and cottages along Terminus Road, such as Kinburn House. James Peerless started a building firm in 1850, which continued, latterly as Peerless Dennis, into the 1930s. With Ebenezer Morris, ironfounder, his name is still on all the lamp-posts, gutters, manhole covers and railings installed in Eastbourne between the 1850s and 1910.

Henry Bradford had established himself as a coal merchant in 1828, with wharves and yards at Seahouses. He was of a long-standing Eastbourne family who continue in the town today. One of his sons, Samuel, realising that the railway would revolutionise the movement of goods, arranged to have a presence at the station from the beginning. At their peak Bradfords had 104 wagons, moved over 500 tons of coal a week, and supplied everyone. John Henry Campion Coles, a solicitor, was clerk to almost everything: the Local Board, the vestry from 1857 to 1883, the final Town Clerk of Pevensey, the Princess Alice Hospital from 1883 to 1914, the Eastbourne Pier Company, the Eastbourne Gas Company, Eastbourne College, the Commissioners of Taxes for Pevensey, and the

Town Clerkship of Eastbourne between 1883 and 1890.

Growth relied upon adequate water and gas (and later electricity) services for residents and visitors. All were dependent on coal, which the railway could supply. The Eastbourne Gas Company, formed in February 1851, had brewer Robert Cooper as its first chairman. The London Brighton and South Coast Railway Company offered a station site for a nominal sum and the Gas Company obliged by importing all its coal by rail rather than by collier from the beach. One firm that suffered as gas became available was H.B. Marchant, candlemakers. The fashion of letting houses for the season was becoming less popular, although it survived into the 1920s, and the larger ones were being taken over by another of Eastbourne's acceptable 'industries' – the private school. An early one was started in the 1850s by the Shoosmith family at The Grove, which closed in 1896 to make way for Grove Road.

In spite of wobbles, the town was entering a period of rapid growth. The population doubled every ten years, and the town 'built by gentlemen for gentlemen' offered opportunities for traders who aimed their wares at those with money and time to spend. One such was master baker Henry Vine who, in 1858, established his own business first in

46 The Princess Alice tree (*c.*1900) was at the concourse that became War Memorial Square. On the right hand corner from 1860 to 1976 was dispensing chemist H.R. Browne, which included a blazing coal fire to greet customers. On the left hand corner of South Street and Cornfield Terrace draper and silk merchant Henry Evenden (1833-93) set up with John Terry. They soon had six live-in staff. The shop became Dickeson & French, and from 1991 the furnisher David Salmon.

47 Eastbourne's oldest postbox, dating from the 1870s, is a wall box in The Goffs opposite Moat Croft Road. Eastbourne's first street box for pre-paid mail was opposite the Leaf Hall, and replaced the Seahouses Receiving Office.

Seaside and later Terminus Road. Twenty years on he had a resident staff of six.

The postal services responded to the new demands.[1] George Cook had taken over the Old Town Ocklynge post office, which served the whole town, although his daughter performed most of the duties. On his death in 1857 this became a sub-post office; by 1875 Mary Cook was appointed postmaster at the main office, at 42 Terminus Road. The Payne family ran the Ocklynge post office into the 20th century. Dorothy Hunt, who helped

48 The Vestry Hall was built in 1851 near the present Central Library, and demolished in 1902 for the Technical Institute. Common vestry meetings had governed the parishes of England for centuries. As towns became larger, and secular affairs more complex, Eastbourne ratepayers voted on whether to have a Local Board instead. Of 259 voters only 111 were for the proposal, but in those days ratepayers had votes in proportion to the value of their properties and the proposal was carried by the multiple votes. The new Local Board met in the Vestry Hall and governed the town from 1859 to 1883.

out, recalls holidaymakers sending 'Arrived Safely' telegrams on Saturday mornings. The new Local Board felt they needed 'a coat of arms' and the *Eastbourne Gazette*, the town's first newspaper, started on 11 July 1859. Beforehand the *Sussex Express* and *Lewes Times* had circulated in the town. The *Eastbourne Chronicle*, which became the *Herald*, appeared in 1865.

There was a Race Course on Bullock Down, and Eastbourne's Regatta was first held on 26 August 1859. A big crowd lined the cliff from Grand Parade to the Wish, and the Regatta became an annual event. The first recorded cricket match was in 1738, probably on the Links, near where Eastbourne College's all-weather pitches are today. From 1858 the Marsh Field, alongside the railway, was the main venue, and it is said that trains pulled up at the ground for visiting teams to alight. This was the scene of the visit of W.G. Grace in 1868, and of the

first touring team, the Aboriginal Blacks, who also gave a demonstration of boomerang throwing.

In 1860 Stephen Bindon started his furniture business in Pevensey Road. The family ran the most exclusive shop in the town, supplying bedding to Compton Place for a visit of the Prince of Wales, later King Edward VII. The same year Richard Francis took over a branch of Parson's stonemasons, and soon had his own Carrara railway sidings, while his brother, William, built much property in Terminus Road, and became a member of the Local Board and the Borough Council. One business that has been carried on since its establishment in 1863 is Leonard Stevens, saddlers, in Crown Street.

Caleb Diplock's Lion Steam Brewery was perhaps the most successful venture. Diplock came to Eastbourne in 1856 and bought a house in Terminus Road which he called *London House*. In 1858 he bought the *Commercial Hotel* (*Diplock's Hotel*), and

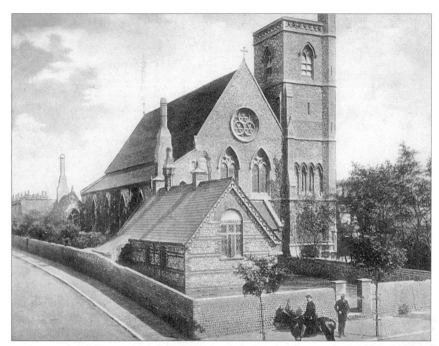

49 Christ Church and Brodie Hall Infants' School, Seaside. Mrs Annie Davies Gilbert donated the land in 1859. Designed by an associate of Pugin, this is not a pretty church externally, being more like a large flint barn. By 1868 additions were necessary and, as it was on shingle, the spire had to be reinforced. There is a memorial window to Princess Alice, and a Willis organ. The Rev. Charles Dodgson (Lewis Carroll) preached here in 1893, not deterred from doing so by his stammer.

50 Meads Road *c.*1895. The cottages on the left, in front of the Town Hall, are on the site of Caffyn's head office today. In 1856 William Morris Caffyn was apprenticed to his uncle Ebenezer Morris to learn the trade of 'ironmonger, tinman and brazier' at two shillings a week. He opened his first shop on 19 May 1865 at the near end of the row, as a gas and hot water fitter.

51 Caleb Diplock's Lion Brewery 'off-licence' in Terminus Road is now the Portman Building Society. The fabric has hardly altered. The Lion Brewery had eight branch offices, a beer bottling department and its own artesian well; the wine cellarage was 'upward of a mile in extent', and there was a mineral water factory in North Street. By 1883 Caleb had sold up and retired with 'a noble fortune', but he died the next year. The brewery closed in the First World War and became the Southdown Bus Station in the 1920s.

52 Frederick Gowland Hopkins PRS (1861-1947), born in Eastbourne and a Nobel Laureate in 1929 for his work on vitamins. He described watching the construction of Eastbourne pier, which so impressed him that he cherished the hope he might share in some similar great enterprise. Having inherited his father's scientific bent, he was invited to Cambridge, but the only way he could make a living was by teaching anatomy. In 1910 Trinity College elected him to a Fellowship. During the 26 years he held it he was never asked for one single service in return, which meant he could give up teaching and concentrate on research, and he became a pioneer in the study of accessory food factors. Professor of Biochemistry at Cambridge from 1914, he was knighted in 1925 and President of the Royal Society from 1930 to 1935. He was particularly proud of his Order of Merit. Max Perutz, a 1987 Nobel Prize winner, said Gowland's reputation decided him on Cambridge.

in 1863 his Brewery and Malt House. This was well and truly christened with a supper for those involved in the building work.[2] 'At six o'clock 135 respectably dressed mechanics sat down to four rounds of beef and a variety of vegetables. Liquor was served *ad lib* from three barrels of beer.' There were toasts to 'The Queen', and to 'The Army, the Navy and the Volunteers'; these were followed by toasts to 'Mr. Diplock', to 'Mr. James Peerless', the builder, and to the architect 'Mr. James Berry', and Mr. Peerless gave a toast to 'All the carpenters and joiners and the stair maker'. Mr Weaver gave 'The Town of Eastbourne' and Mr John Maynard

gave 'Prosperity to the Lion Brewery'; Mr Diplock gave the 'Health of the brewer, the cooper, and the maltster' and, in a separate toast, 'The Press'. There were responses to all these toasts, with Mr Doig, proprietor of the *Eastbourne Gazette*, giving the toast 'May good feeling ever exist between employer and employed', whereupon 'The Ladies' and 'The health of Master Caleb Diplock', then 21, were proposed. It seems only fitting that one of the last toasts was to the 'Foreman Plasterer'.

In 1861 Drs William Abbot Smith and Charles Hayman wrote the booklet *Eastbourne ... a resort for invalids*. The Marine Parade library had been taken

53 Eastbourne seafront from the pier *c*.1900, showing an Allchorn sailing boat off for a trip round the bay. The family started their pleasure boat service in 1861. Cruises operated in season from near the pier to Beachy Head lighthouse, and there was also a round trip to Birling Gap and the Crumbles. The rowing boats in the foreground would be Sayer's, another Eastbourne firm sold to Allchorn's in 1964.

over in 1857 by Frederick Hopkins, a cousin of the Misses Hopkins and of Gerard Manley Hopkins, and a recognised amateur scientist who had married Elizabeth Gowland. He died from scarlet fever shortly after their only child, Frederick Gowland, was born, so Elizabeth's brother, Thomas Stafford Gowland, came to run the shop.[3] He partook of a daily swim off the pier into his 70s.

The first photographer was Albert Vidler in 1861. He worked from 86 South Street, but doesn't appear to have been a success and he returned to his day job of surveying.[4] George and Rebecca Lavis were the best-known Eastbourne photographers, although T.B. Rowe took most of their pictures. Before long photographers were plentiful, William Hicks, George Churchill, Rudolph Vieler and William Kent among them.

Thomas Hopley set up a school at 22 Grand Parade for the sons of gentlemen. He was a severe disciplinarian, but successful, and published

54 A wonderful collection of top hats for the opening of Eastbourne's first sewer at Langney on 3 May 1867. The Duke of Devonshire is in light-coloured trousers, G.A. Wallis is three to his left, Canon Thomas Pitman is to his right, and behind him is J.H. Campion Coles. Dr C. Hayman is to the right of John Gosden, who wears grey trousers and watch chain. It was most appropriate that the Duke attended, for the town ran out of money and he paid to finish the job. *The Lancet* of 11 May 1867 thought, 'the health of the town will be much improved'.

pamphlets advocating physical exercise and chastisement to harden children. There were only six pupils, all sent because of special needs, and on 21 April 1860 Reginald Cancellor, 14, a backward lad with 'bad habits', was called to Hopley's study following 'intransigence' and beaten for two hours. The next morning the boy was found dead, but the inquest verdict was natural causes.[5] The following day the boy's brother came to Eastbourne, saw bruises on the body and demanded a post-mortem, and when this showed horrifying injuries Hopley was arrested, charged with manslaughter, found guilty and sentenced to four years. At the trial the Lord Chief Justice laid down that any parent or schoolmaster had a right to beat a boy, but in moderation and never in anger. Amazingly, there were people who thought Hopley had suffered 'a most remarkable injustice'.[6]

After 1860 the *Burlington* bought up the leases of the Grand Parade houses on both sides, and by 1938 the entire western end had been added to the hotel. In 1923 number 5 became the *Claremont Hotel* and by 1951 the hotel occupied the whole eastern end.

In 1863 property values dropped following a scarlet fever epidemic, and the eastern end of the town began to be developed. Drs Hall and Hayman advised that the town should have proper drainage, and the result was the first sewage outfall at Langney Point. It was not one of Wallis's successes and needed modifying.

Similarly, shortly after the station opened it was realised that it was cramped and in the wrong place, and the platforms were extended in 1860. Meanwhile, the Duke and Carew Davies Gilbert swapped parcels of land so that their planned developments

55 This view from St Saviour's spire looking west, *c.*1873, shows the College nearby, Cliffe House, or Earp's Folly, on the skyline, and St John's Church, Meads on the right. William Earp's folly was built in 1870 on the Ravenscroft site, with all the flues drawn to one chimney in a tower. In the same year the Duke of Devonshire sent £1,000 to erect St Saviour's spire. At the ceremony to fix the weather vane on 10 September 1872 the congregation assembled at the north porch, singing 'Pleasant are thy Courts above', while the vicar, the Rev. H.R. Whelpton, positioned the vane. It blew down shortly afterwards and was never replaced.

could proceed. The Davies Gilberts wished to construct a new approach to their estate to by-pass Old Town's narrow roads, steep hills and awkward corners. The station, however, lay in the middle of the projected route, Upperton Road, so in 1866 it was moved and rebuilt in much the same place as now. The Avenue, another of the Davies Gilbert plans made possible by moving the railway station, was laid out by Nicholas Whitley, the Davies Gilbert agent and noted local historian. In 1904 Whitley Bridge was named after him and his son, Michell.

The Gas Company moved in 1869 from the station to Lottbridge Drove, already connected to the Ballast Line. By now rail was essential not only to bring in coal, but also to dispatch the by-products: sulphate of ammonia for fertilisers, creosote for builders, and coke and ash for road making and

filter beds. The railway company extended their goods yard over the old gas works site, and before long the Gas Company had to buy an extra 10 acres of land from the Duke.

On 6 June 1865 Dr Hayman proposed a 'Proprietary College to Educate the Sons of Noblemen and Gentlemen'. With the Duke's support, on 20 August 1867 Eastbourne College in Spencer Road admitted 15 boys under the Rev. James Russell Wood as headmaster.

One of the first local artisans to achieve success was Henry Sutton. An astute businessman from a shoemaking family, he branched out in 1861 as manager of the *Railway Hotel* on the corner of Terminus Road and Cornfield Road. The building of Upperton Road meant that the *Gilbert Arms* (*The Squirrel*) had also to be demolished and Sutton,

56 Edward Walker, an Australian, bought an estate at Oxted and a town house in London. For his seaside home he built Araluen in 1870 at 36 Grand Parade, a large family house with a garden which he needed for his 17 children from two marriages. It is now the *Cumberland Hotel*. It was said that he named Larkin's Field, adjoining the Saffrons, and that he made his money from sheep farming, but the name Araluen is associated with the Australian gold rush.

sensing an opportunity, acquired a plot near the station and built the *Gildredge Hotel*, to which the *Gilbert* licence was transferred in 1870. He became a Freemason and an Alderman, with a farm at Horam Road.

The church of St Saviour and St Peter in South Street is accepted as the finest Victorian church in the town, and the graceful broach spire at 176 ft. [54m.] the loftiest. Designed by G.E. Street in Gothic style, its site was given, as usual, by the Duke of Devonshire, and on 17 October 1865 the foundation stone was laid in a turnip field. Built by James Peerless, the £20,000 cost was paid by G. Whelpton and his son and grandson were the first vicars. A purpose-built hall by D. Clarke was completed in 1957. The wealth generated by Whelpton's

Pills is an example, along with Holloway's Potions and Beecham's Powders, of how well the purveyors of useless restoratives fared in Victorian times.

On 29 May 1867 Father Charles Patrick King arrived in Eastbourne to take up his pastoral duties, with his sister as housekeeper. There were only half a dozen Catholics in the town, and he held services in the basement of his house in Ceylon Place. In 1868 the church moved to Junction Road, and the next year he built Stella Maris Church for £450 at his own expense. Emma Brodie was instrumental in persuading the Duke to give £1,000 towards the cost of St John the Evangelist Church in Meads, which was built in 1869 by James Peerless. In the early years, St John's and its vicar, the Rev. Edward Adams, enjoyed isolation, and Adams

57 The 1890s workhouse, showing the inmates in standard uniform. By 1900 it was realised that people were in workhouses only because they were infirm or could not get work. Helped by publicity, such as Sim's ballads, public opinion switched and conditions eased. In Eastbourne trained nurses were appointed from 1875, an Infirmary ward was built in 1889, and the children went to outside schools and even had treats. The stigma, however, persisted into the middle of the 20th century, when old folk would plead not to be sent into the 'pauper hospital'.

58 Blanche, Countess of Burlington's school in Meads. Blanche (1812-40) was the 7th Duke's wife. The inscription reads, 'So teach us to number our days, That we may apply our hearts unto wisdom'. The attractive flint building was a school into the 1900s. Four ladies provided elementary infant schools to keep the cost off the ratepayers. This was the first, in 1836; Lydia Brodie (1815-91) provided the second in 1853, now Flint Halls; the third was the infants' school next to Christ Church by Julia Brodie (1814-72); and, finally, Maria Brodie (1807-92) started one, now Meads County Primary.

59 All Saints' Convalescent Hospital (centre) and Meads from Beachy Head way in the 1890s. St Luke's Children's Hospital (knocked down in the 1960s for Dolphin Court) is mid-right, and St Andrew's School (formerly Colstock's Farm) mid-left.

was able to hone up his chess skills sufficiently to play countywide. In the 20 years after 1871 the population trebled from 11,000 and Eastbourne joined up with Meads. It was said of Meads in 1890, 'meadows and cornfields have become studded with stately villas and beautiful gardens', and in 1904 the *Eastbourne Chronicle* referred to it as 'the unrivalled Belgravia of a salubrious and flourishing health resort'.

Not far from 'Belgravia' was Eastbourne's workhouse. The lines, *It is Christmas day in the Workhouse*, were by George Robert Sims, a journalist who went to the Grove School and had a house in the town, where perhaps he saw *the* workhouse.[8] The diet was monotonous. Breakfast and supper menus for males in the 1880s consisted of 8oz. of bread and one pint of gruel. For females, and children over seven years of age, 6oz. of bread and one pint of gruel, and younger children 6oz. bread and ½ pint gruel. At dinner time men got half a pound of bread and 1½oz. of cheese, women 6oz. of bread and 1½oz. of cheese, and young children made do on 4oz. bread and one ounce of cheese.[9]

Inmates were given a series of graduated exercises entitled 'A Schedule of Tasks of Work'. Males had to break 12cwt. of flints per day – so you can see the justification for positive bread discrimination. The able-bodied women had to pick 2½lb. unbeaten oakum or 5lb. beaten oakum a day in summer, or 2lb. and 4lb. in the winter.[10] They could opt instead for 10 hours washing or scrubbing. Old folk chopped wood for the fires. Many workhouses introduced a starvation diet for nine days after delivery of single women as 'a deterrent against the use of the workhouse as a place to be confined'. It was said of the Eastbourne workhouse, 'erring women who have been driven to seek the cold shelter of the workhouse walls in their hour of need have been excluded from any participation in the trifling luxuries afforded to the inmates at the joyous season of Christmas'.[11]

Children outside the workhouse fared little better. Although the government gave grants for the education of the poorer classes, the only elementary schooling in Eastbourne was at St Mary's and Holy Trinity Churches. It was joined by St Andrew's

60   De Walden House was built by Lucy Joan Cavendish-Bentinck, daughter of the 4th Duke of Portland, a second cousin of the Duke of Devonshire, and widow of Charles Augustus Ellis, 6th Lord Howard de Walden. Oxford Street, Harley Street and Portland Place were a tiny part of the family wealth. Lucy also built de Walden Lodge, in Meads Road, and the Meads Institute, now Meads Club. When the Water Company tried to charge her £30 she had a £1,000 well sunk in this garden. In 1889 she moved to another of her houses at West Malvern, where she died aged 93. It is said she bequeathed her corsets to her maid, 'As she always had such a poor figure'.

School Norway, St Joseph's RC School at Whitley Road and a Methodist school in Susans Road. Such private generosity kept the rates down, but it was storing up trouble. Eastbourne College decided to move from its temporary quarters when the Duke of Devonshire made land available in Meads, with Larkfield House for the headmaster's residence. The buildings of 1870 were Henry Currey's first major work in Eastbourne, and he made additions in 1877. The school grew slowly until, in 1888, the Rev. Dr. Charles Crowden came in with 90 new pupils.

Eastbourne Ladies' College, in Grassington Road in 1870, was Eastbourne's first purpose-built girls' school. The building was taken over by Eastbourne College and renamed Pennell House, after an Old Boy holder of the V.C., but demolished in 1987. Other schools were moving to the healthy town.

Clifton House School was brought by the Rev. Edward Crake from Oxfordshire to South Street in 1868. It flourished and moved to a new site in The Avenue. Twenty years or so later Peter and Douglas Gilbert moved their school, Roborough, into The Avenue building, where Sir Alec Guinness was a pupil. This school lasted into the Second World War.

Eastbourne was well supplied with churches and private schools, but anyone involved with the Petty Sessions had to travel to Hailsham until two local magistrates, Reginald Graham and Leonard Willard, inaugurated a weekly sitting in the Vestry Hall in the 1860s, and from 1887 in the Town Hall.[12] After 1911 the town had its separate Bench in accord with the new County Borough status.

The Eastbourne Pier Company Ltd., registered on 3 April 1865 with £15,000 capital, provided

61   The Duke of Devonshire's Orchestra gave its first concert at the Winter Garden in 1876 under conductor
Julian Adams. After he left, in 1887, Norfolk Megone conducted in the summer (when it was called the
Devonshire Park Orchestra), and Pierre Tas in the winter. The orchestra had over fifty players and set the tone
in musical entertainment. Appearing with it were many music makers, including Fritz Kreisler, Jan Paderewski,
Jan Kubelik, John McCormack, Solomon, Clara Butt, Maggie Teyte and Myra Hess. It was taken over by the
Council after the First World War.

the landing stage demanded of every proper resort.
In the days when recovery from a broken leg or
pneumonia entailed months of convalescence, any
town boasting of its health-giving properties hosted
a convalescent hospital, so Eastbourne was delighted
when the All Saints' Convalescent Hospital, run by
Anglican Sisters, opened.[13] Visitors at this time
included Edward Lear, the artist and author of
limericks, who visited a number of times, being a
friend of the Lushington family. He painted a view
of Beachy Head. Pianist and composer William
Sterndale Bennett also came frequently.

'A good many buildings are going on or will
shortly begin', so the Duke of Devonshire wrote
tersely of Eastbourne in his 1873 diary. The
Cavendish Hotel had opened, and no doubt he was
referring to Devonshire Park, designed for 'high
class recreation', and part of a greater scheme to
extend the holiday season. The site at the junction
of Carlisle and College Roads had been left empty
because of its marshy nature, and the Devonshire
Park and Baths Company was formed in 1874, the
Duke providing the land and £16,000, for which
he received half the shares. The swimming baths
opened in 1874. Built by G.A. Wallis, they were
the largest heated salt-water baths in the country,
the separate ladies' and gentlemen's baths being

filled and emptied by the tidal rise and fall of the
sea and heated to 70°F, although the sea water
wasn't always replaced at each tide and tended to
become algid. Admission was 6d. in 1918. The
Floral Hall opened in 1875 and the Pavilion the
next year, both designed by Henry Currey. The
Winter Garden seated 2,000 and continues to be
used for concerts, balls, shows and receptions. The
Park had a music garden and facilities for cricket,
tennis, racquets, roller skating, and cycling, and
tennis championships have been staged there since
the 19th century.

The Devonshire Park Theatre, also by Currey,
opened in 1884 and is described by H. Clunn as
'one of the finest on the south coast'. It is delightfully ornate inside, and the Italianate towers house
the fire escapes. The oriental-style public bar in
Compton Street, now the *Buccaneer*, was built by
the Devonshire Park Company in 1897, possibly to
ape the Indian Pavilion of 1891. The *Eastbourne
Gazette* was bought in 1873 by T.R. Beckett, whose
son, Arthur, started that fund of Sussex lore, the
Sussex County Magazine, in 1926.

Two different schools were begun in the 1870s.
In 1872 the nonconformist New College was
founded by Frederick Schreiner in Spencer Road
and in 1888 it moved to Ellesmere, Compton Place

62   The *Grand Hotel* in 1890. When it opened in 1877 there were only six bathrooms for 200 rooms, although chambermaids carried up hot water twice a day. Extensions were required in 1888. The original E-shape arms were joined up along Compton Street to give shops at street level and hotel rooms above. At numbers 8 and 9 there were Turkish Baths from 1889 to the 1920s.

Road. It folded after Schreiner's death, the buildings becoming Temple Grove School; today they house the Dental Practice Agency. Moira House, a Girls' Boarding & Day School, was founded in 1875 in Upper Carlisle Road. Former pupils include actresses Susannah Corbett, Prunella Scales and Sarah Woodward, playwright Mona Swann, and Rumer Godden, the author of over fifty novels.

On 28 May 1875 William Earp, a builder, applied to build the *Grand Hotel* on King Edward's Parade, and he became the first manager. The architect was R.K. Blessley.[14] Henry Currey was architect of the

Queen's Hotel, Marine Parade, which opened in 1880. It marked the start of the eastern working-class part of the town, for before 1939 it was said that no lady would walk east of the *Queen's Hotel*.

The Eastbourne Bicycle Club was formed in 1877. There were about 180 members, with 30 ladies, and the club was said to be a matrimonial agency. There were weekly runs to Lewes and Hastings, and in 1896 John Niedermayer took a party from Brussels to Bonn, 450 miles by bike. 'There was disappointment with the continental breakfasts and the members would reorder to

THE GRAPHIC

AN ILLUSTRATED WEEKLY·NEWSPAPER

NO. 710.—VOL. XXVIII.
Reg.ᵈ at General Post Office as a Newspaper]   SATURDAY, JULY 7, 1883   WITH EXTRA SUPPLEMENT [PRICE SIXPENCE   Or by Post Sixpence Halfpenny

1. Waiting for the Prince, Terminus Road.—2. View of the Princess Alice Memorial Hospital.—3. The Opening Ceremony : Presenting Purses.—4. The Arch of Nets and Boats.
THE OPENING OF THE PRINCESS ALICE MEMORIAL HOSPITAL BY THE PRINCE AND PRINCESS OF WALES AT EASTBOURNE

63 The opening of the Princess Alice Hospital, on 30 June 1883, by the Prince and Princess of Wales. Clockwise: the procession in Terminus Road; the hospital; the opening ceremony, with presentation of purses; and a fishermen's arch. Princess Christian paid the first official royal visit to Eastbourne in 1882 to lay the foundation stone. Princess Alice, Queen Victoria's second daughter, had spent a holiday at Eastbourne in 1878 and so impressed the townspeople that when she died of diphtheria, a few weeks later, aged 35, they were determined to perpetuate her memory and raised enough by public subscriptions for a cottage hospital.

appease their appetites.' It prospered until the Second World War, but afterwards the club had to sell its base, Ashampstead, and in 1991 it was wound up. Bicycling didn't do Niedermayer any harm for he died aged 96 in 1953.

Following yet more church building, there was a suggestion that Eastbourne had more church seats per head of the population than any other town. They varied from a 'tin' Immanuel Church in Hyde Road, a protest at St Saviour's 'Romanising incense-burning tendencies', to All Souls' Church, set on an island in Susans Road and constructed in Lombardo-Byzantine style with a free-standing campanile.

'In order to assist those anxious to help themselves', the Eastbourne Temperance Building Society was incorporated in 1877 and an Artisans' Dwelling Company was started in 1885. The aim was to build four- or five-roomed cottages for letting to families at a rent equal to what they were paying for two substandard rooms, and over the next decade or two a number of houses were erected to fulfil the company's rôle.

A Seaside coffee house, *Ye Rising Sun,* was opened in 1879 by Wilhelmina Brodie Hall as a 'boon to the working classes', but really to combat 'the demon drink'. She wrote, 'I am opposed to treating such ventures as philanthropy, and apart from the initial investment it was an ordinary commercial business'. It was a success, lasting until 1924. Coffee stalls were also run by the Church of England Temperance Society at sites including 'Memorial Square', where one went on serving until 1940. The workmen brought their horses along, and William Mitchell, the stall keeper, would store stale bread for them. One man would order a cup of coffee for himself and one for his mate, his donkey, who would drink it out of the cup after it had cooled.

Wilhelmina, a clever grand-daughter of the Rev. Brodie, helped foster out children, among them the 7- and 11-year-old brothers of George Meek, Eastbourne's 'bathchairman'. She persuaded the Guardians to send pauper children to Canada where they appear to have done well, with one exception, an 18-year-old boy convicted of murder. When she heard she looked up her records and found evidence of insanity in the family, so wired this information to Saskatchewan and the sentence was commuted to 10 years' imprisonment. On his release she placed him in a job and by 1904 he was doing well. She looked after her charges.

Electricity first illuminated the Floral Hall in 1881, the year the population reached 21,000. Less than forty per cent of local people were born in Eastbourne and over fifty per cent came from outside Sussex. The next year the Eastbourne Electric Light Company was formed and leased the old Bedfordwell water works, moving in 1884 to Junction Road. The town's first public electric lighting was seen on 4 September 1882, five hours before New York's was switched on.

The oldest surviving soccer club in the town, and probably in Sussex, was formed at Devonshire Park and played its first match against Clifton House School on 26 October 1881. The club moved to the Saffrons ground when that opened and changed its name to Eastbourne Town three years later.

Visitors to the town included Karl Marx, founder of international communism, but when a plaque was put up to him it was torn down. Richard Blackmore, the novelist, also came for holidays, and Sir Rowland Hill, the advocate of a uniform pre-paid postage rate and national ownership of the railways, in 1867, took the train. Among the school-boys at Kent House School in Staveley Road was E.M. Forster.

The year 1883 was the town's coming of age. Eastbourne's Charter of Incorporation was granted on 16 June, elections followed on 1 November, and the first meeting of the Borough of Eastbourne was held on 9 November. George Ambrose Wallis, the Duke's agent and Eastbourne's Mr Fix-It, had respectability thrust upon him when he was elected the first mayor. The first celebration of a busy year had been in the February, when eight Eastbourne ringers rang a true touch of grandsire triples, the number of changes representing 1883. The telegraph lines were extended, and the first telephone exchange opened in Grove Road. The *Albion Hotel* had number 1, which it carried until automation in 1966. In 1895 telephones were installed in the Town Hall, fire station and police station, and the exchange, catering for over 100 subscribers, moved to the corner of Grove Road and Hyde Road. Installation cost £3 10s. and a local call was 1d. New businesses were also starting up and one which has survived is Charlwood's the jewellers.

The year also saw Eastbourne's most famous lifeboat rescue. On 25 November a barque, the *New Brunswick,* was in distress near Birling Gap. Realising that the lifeboat could not make way in the teeth of one of the worst SSW gales in memory, it was decided to haul the *William and Mary* overland some five miles. At the Gap the boat was launched into a violent sea and, under coxswain Charlie 'Bones' Hide, was able to rescue the crew of the barque.

In a dense fog, unusual for Eastbourne, the sea wall round the Redoubt was extended, the keystone being laid on 4 January 1884 by G.A. Wallis. The sea had made great inroads east of the pier in 1878, and after work started 900ft. of the new wall was washed away in May 1880. After completion the Duke and Carew Davies Gilbert conveyed to the fishermen an alternative fishing station east of the Redoubt; west of the pier the Duke was shaping the Parades at his own expense. Fishing remained a dangerous job and in November 1893 the fishing

64 The Town Hall by S.G. Kirk, 1888, described by Pevsner as 'free Renaissance'. It was built in Grove Road, on the site of Stocks' Bank (Mr Thomas' house), but only after much argument over site, architect and builder. Finally designed by W.T. Foulkes and built by James Peerless, the foundation stone was laid by Lord Edward Cavendish on 9 October 1884. It was opened by the mayor on 20 October 1886. The site cost £3,000 and the building £35,000. This painting has no clock, because it wasn't installed until 1892.

boat *Thistle* was lost off Beachy Head. Fishing families were already diversifying, and in 1884 W. & W. Erridge paid £20 a year for permission to place deckchairs on Grand Parade.

In the early 1880s Robert Campbell, a Scot, brought to the town the concept of eating out, and his dining rooms in Compton Street prospered. With George Brown he formed the Eastbourne Scottish Pipe Band, which celebrated its centenary in 1996. The Eastbourne Market Company built

an arcade in Grove Road, which opened in 1888, but in 1904 it was wound up.

The Eastbourne parliamentary constituency came into being as a result of the 1885 Boundary Commission report. It had been in the Sussex constituency, and in the 1857 General Election the few Eastbourne voters had been taken to Lewes by carriage.

The new Town Hall tower by Gillett & Johnson had space for a four-dial clock and bells. It remained

65   The railway station *c*.1890. Eastbourne's third, it was completed in 1886. The design, by F.D. Bannister, is a mixture of styles with a dominant clock tower (left by the tree); the canopies and ornamental cast-iron columns are typical railway architecture. The coat of arms on the tower mixes those of the City of London, Portsmouth and Hastings, the LB&SCR limits.

empty, delayed by the cost, until noon on 11 July 1892, when the £700 Westminster chiming clock was started by the mayor. The chimes are Cambridge quarters.

The Saffrons, the sports ground along Saffrons Road, had opened in 1886 together with the adjacent Larkin's Field. The name comes from the crocus grown at nearby Saffron Gardens. Over the years the Eastbourne Saffrons Sports Club has offered archery, athletics, bowls, cricket, croquet, football, hockey, squash and table-tennis. The main pavilion was built in 1889, at a cost of £600, but has since been modernised and expanded – and twice burnt down.

The Royal Eastbourne Golf Club was granted its title in the October of 1887.[15] It was the first club in the county, along with Seaford. The Duke of Devonshire granted permission to use the Links

and a nine-hole course was laid out so as to interfere as little as possible with the sheep grazing tenancy. The following year an independent Ladies' Club was formed which became the Royal Ladies' Golf Club.

When Canon Thomas Pitman, the autocratic low church vicar of Eastbourne, died on 13 May 1890, aged 89, the town mourned and Eastbourne's shops closed.[16] None had an ill word to say of him. He was involved in all the town's events, and diaries of the time assiduously record his daily rounds and the minutiae of his health – assuming, that is, 'Vicar better' refers to his medical state, not his sermons! When George Ambrose Wallis, representative of corporate Eastbourne, had his portrait painted, Pitman's was painted by public subscription.

66   The Salvation Army came to Eastbourne in 1890 and opened their Citadel in Langney Road. The organisation was welcomed, but some people were irritated when the band broke the 1885 Eastbourne Improvement Act by marching and playing on a Sunday. Skirmishes broke out and attempts to stop the band were made by the 'Skeleton Army', probably louts encouraged by publicans worried over the possibility of stricter licensing laws, although the mayor was also against the Army. The culmination came on 19 July 1891 with the arrest of members of the Camberwell Band, come to lend encouragement. In 1892 the Salvation Army promoted a bill to change the law.

When the Salvation Army came to Eastborne instruments were trampled and clothes torn off; the violence was a reaction against strangers coming into the county and attempting to change the ways of a lifetime. At least Eastbourne, unlike Worthing, didn't have to call in the armed forces to restore order.

It is often claimed the town had 365 schools. It was indubitably a centre of education, but there is no evidence for such a number at any one time; even G.F. Chambers' claim of 200 in 1894 is an exaggeration, although we may not know about every school. Southdown College, for example, moved five times, and many small private schools came and went over the years; a multiplicity of crammers, with half-a-dozen pupils, changed site and name every term. In 1877 there were 13 boys' and 13 girls' schools or colleges in Eastbourne, 34 and 47 in 1897, and by 1911 there were 37 schools for girls and 45 for boys. Even into the 1930s families moved to Eastbourne simply because of the choice of schools, and Meads was the ideal centre, with so many villas suitable for conversion.

Such schools did not provide universal education for Eastbourne's children and a vestry meeting in December 1872 decided to provide additional places by subscriptions and private benefactions, but Eastbourne was one of only two authorities in England and Wales that did not have a School Board. Wishing to encourage more residents, the Local Board was reluctant to increase the rates and, for their own reasons, the churches and ratepayers preferred to hold bazaars to raise funds. Hence Eastbourne's elementary education was by church schools, generous gifts of land and money by wealthy churchgoers providing the 656 extra places required. School treats were annual highlights. One year 336 schoolchildren marched to the station to go to Pevensey and be joined by others to the total of 550. At the end of a day of games and tea, and exhausted teachers, each child was given a bun and an orange.

67 Lewis Carroll (1832-98) stayed with the Dyer family at 7 Lushington Road (left) and at 2 Bedfordwell Road over 22 summers between 1876 and 1897. Born Charles Lutwidge Dodgson, he was a mathematics lecturer at Oxford University, and, of course, a photographer and author of *Alice in Wonderland* and *Through the Looking Glass*. At least one of his books, *Sylvie and Bruno*, was written in Eastbourne, and it showed the town's influence, evincing a heavy patina of social morality. Mrs Dyer was 'a good motherly creature', and Dodgson occupied 'a nice little front sitting room and adjoining bedroom'; he brought his own tin bath.

68 The metal licence plate at the base of the stone wall on King Edward's Parade marked the Saddled Donkey Stand. The WD-stone (centre) was the eastern extent of the War Department's land. Licence plates found around the town, about 15cm. across, indicate where a licensed conveyance could ply for hire under an Act of 1840. In 1893 there were some 100 horse/hackney carriage stands (HCS), four goat chaise (GCS), two saddled pony (SPS), 60 luggage porter (LPS) and 50 BCS. Finally an MCS – motor charabanc stand – appeared.

69 Frances Jardine describes the entertainment at the turn of the century. 'The Minstrels gave two performances a day, and there was a Punch and Judy show at the pier.' Beachy Head, the beach and the sea remained the top attractions, but the Pierrot Concert Parties were ousting the Minstrels.

The growth of Eastbourne brought demands that were beyond the finances of the church. By the 1890s there was again a deficiency of school places, and the town signally failed to comply with the Technical Instruction Act of 1889. In response the Borough Council set up in 1898 the Eastbourne Voluntary Schools Building Co. to build Willowfield School. The Education Act of 1902 abolished School Boards, made local authorities responsible for education, and provided for scholarships to grammar schools. The Council became a Local Education Authority and bought (back) the new Willowfield Infants and Higher Grade Schools for £5,995 (plus £517 for fittings) in 1904. The first year the education charge was on the rates it hit 3¾d. in the £1, ratepayers declaring that the committee would 'spend and spend'.

Harry Swift recounts that he left school at 13 in the 1890s for his first job as a page boy at the *Grand Hotel*. His uniform had a row of brass buttons down his bumfreezer jacket and a smart pill-box hat, and one of his jobs was to light the gas lamps with a tallow taper.

When the 7th Duke died in 1891 the population was 34,969, and the old order was going, slowly. Mr. F.A. Banks records that, 'From the top of Kings Avenue in 1891 cornfields stretched to the marshes, when a fox followed by the Eastbourne Hunt came into Mill Road. The Hurst's Ocklynge Manor gate was open and fox, hounds, and huntsmen rushed in, and out at the back.' Eastbourne's economy had moved from agriculture in 1800 to tourism and education within a century. Apart from civic amenities no industry had been introduced, for no visitor wanted factory chimneys, but this meant seasonal unemployment and pockets of poverty.

The new Borough Police force appeared on 5 April 1891. Comprising one chief constable, two inspectors, six sergeants and 29 constables, the total salaries were £2,870 per annum. The town had

70   The *James Stevens 6* lifeboat (in front) and the *Olive* in the old lifeboathouse. The foundation stone of a new lifeboathouse near the Wish Tower was laid by the Duchess of Devonshire on 16 July 1898. It was named after William Terriss (1847-97), an actor with a love of the sea and an affection for the town, who had been murdered in London the previous December. The cost of £1,126 was met by public subscription. It was the ideal site for the subscribers to inspect their good deed, but in the wrong place for those who manned the lifeboat, for they lived well to the east. From 1903 the *James Stevens No 6* (1899-1924) and *Olive* (1903-21) worked in tandem. The Terriss boathouse was used only for demonstrations after 1924, and on 22 March 1937 it became Britain's first Lifeboat Museum.

had just two beadles before PC Joseph Carter appeared as the sole Eastbourne policeman in 1842, on a salary of £46 6s. a year, although the total supplied by the county had reached 30 by 1890. Eastbourne's first policewoman was not appointed until May 1921.

After a recession in the late 1880s business boomed in the 1890s. Dicker's Stores of Grove Road became the leading grocer in the town, supplying Compton Place, and after Edwin Dicker retired in 1902 Elliott's Stores, founded in 1885 by Herbert Elliott at the corner of South Street and College Road, took his place. Older residents always mention Elliott's coffee grinder and the wonderful aroma. Another high-class provisions purveyor was Cave Austin.

An Eastbourne smallpox epidemic between August and December 1895 gave rise to 15 cases and two deaths. It silenced opposition to the £1,250 cost of building a Smallpox Isolation Hospital on

the Crumbles, near Martello Tower 65. Mrs Olive Bartholomew (née Poole) says she was there about three months, 'behind high wire fencing like a POW camp. We were not allowed visitors, and I had to have all my clothes fumigated.'

Thomas Henry Huxley, biologist and Fellow of the Royal Society, resided in Staveley Road, Meads, between 1890 and 1895. Darwin needed a protagonist for his theory of evolution and Huxley it was who expounded the received form of Darwinism. He coined the term 'agnostic'. A regular visitor until his death, also in 1895, was Friedrich Engels, who collaborated with Karl Marx on *The Communist Manifesto*. In accordance with his wishes his ashes were scattered from Beachy Head.

George Ambrose Wallis died the same year. Agent for the Duke, he ran the Cavendish Estate, and his brother, William Lumb Wallis, ran a building firm. A handy arrangement. His Devonshire Park Baths and the tiered Parades were incredible

71 'For 6d. we occupied a bathing machine for half-an-hour. Each machine had a rope and you were supposed to hang on to prevent drowning. The bathing woman would yell "Hold the rope ladies" regardless of whether we could swim or not. As the tide turned the machine was pulled up the shingle by a horse. The bathing woman would shout "'old tight", an essential warning, for the whole machine rocked from side to side. Goodness knows why there were no accidents. A band played on the beach morning and afternoon for those who preferred not to risk their lives in the bathing machines.'

achievements in the days of spades and wheelbarrows. He built mansions, Holywell Mount, The Links, Clovelly and Fairfield Court, of which only Clovelly in Carlisle Road and The Links remain, converted into flats. The first mayor of Eastbourne, some say he died just in time to save his reputation, but while he was in all likelihood involved in shady deals he was a brilliantly innovative civil engineer and capable manager.

In 1896 Mr J.H. Hardcastle was appointed Eastbourne's first Borough Librarian, and the library opened in the Vestry Hall, Grove Road on 7 July. The Queen's Diamond Jubilee in 1897 was a time for sports days and teas. The Eastbourne Bowling Club was founded at the Saffrons, and the Willingdon Golf Club at Ratton started with nine

72 'In the summer we went in the sea near the Wish Tower. Our 1900 bathing costumes were most decent: my mother's reached to her ankles with a skirt to the knees with frills and the long sleeves had frills at the wrist; my rather daring model ended at the elbows and knees.'

73 *York House Hotel c.*1905. On 1 August 1896 *York House*, at 17 and 18 Royal Parade, was opened as a boarding establishment by Susannah Barratt and her daughter Sarah. The first year's turnover was £156. When Sarah died in 1930 three of her children took over. The hotel was closed and sustained some damage in the war; it fell to Alan and Effie Williamson to return in Easter 1945 and recreate the business. Their son, Matthew, took over in 1972 and the hotel celebrated its centenary in 1996. In 1896 the summer tariff was £1 10s. to £2 2s. 6d. a week, and 'there was none of these 'ere overnight stops or weekend breaks'.

holes. The coup was the 1897-8 mayoralty of the 8th Duke of Devonshire, a national figure.

Although the Parades and Upper Duke's Drive were finished and paid for, and the Devonshire Park complex prospered, Spencer Compton, the 8th Duke (1833-1908), was unhappy about his investment in Eastbourne and offered the Devonshire Park Company to the Borough Council, but the idea was shelved. The Cavendishes were withdrawing their wholehearted financial support for commercial ventures. The 8th Duke, known as an astute politician – and a womaniser – had to cut the family losses, which he did by selling off unwanted land and putting the money into shares.[17] The seaside resorts were moving away from being a substitute spa. For some romantics, like Charlotte Brontë, who fainted at her first sight of the sea, the resorts were still a novelty, but for most they were

an escape, and after the spread of the railways it was increasingly the middle and lower classes who sampled their delights. Young men with telescopes ogling the bathers were a nuisance at many resorts although naturally not at Eastbourne, despite the young ladies wearing the new healthy corsets which by chance uplifted the bust and improved the bottom. Increasingly the seaside developed its own life of piers, promenades and Pierrot shows and the upper classes drifted away to the Riviera.

Despite recurrent over-ambitious property speculations, Eastbourne-upon-Sea had grown faster than any other south coast town in the second half of 19th century. By 1900 it was the largest town in Sussex after Brighton. The Earl of Burlington had been right, Eastbourne had increased its prospects considerably, and perhaps the best was yet to come.

Four

Solid Respectability 1900-1938

The 'Snoot Parade', as it was called by those unlikely to take part, was on the Western Lawns, an expanse of smooth grass in front of the *Grand Hotel*, which had become the place where visiting Edwardians paraded. The craze lasted into the 1930s, as ladies and gentlemen showed they could afford staff to cook their lunch, and there was always the chance that one of their exquisitely finished daughters might catch the eye of a suitor. The Lawns opened in 1883 to a design by Henry Currey, and were conveyed to the Council in 1902 by the 8th Duke of Devonshire, whose 1910 bronze on granite statue stands in the centre. He has removed his pince-nez for no member of the landed class watched such flummery.

Eastbourne had arrived, and the Corporation aimed to keep it that way. In 1901 a proposal by the LB&SCR to move their locomotive and carriage works from Brighton to Eastbourne was halted in its tracks by a majority of the councillors, who considered that invasion by several hundred railway workers would be detrimental to the town's image.

On 1 January 1900 the Eastbourne Electric Light Co. was bought for £82,135. The following year the company had 516 customers paying 4d. a unit (heat) and 2d. (light); by 1933 the respective rates were 1½d. and ½d. for 14,400 customers. Electric lighting for the pier was installed by Percy and Harry Caffyn in 1901. They had joined their father's gas business in 1892 but branched out into electrical appliances. Another family firm that has prospered is Walter Llewellyn & Sons. Walter and William Llewellyn started as jobbing builders in December 1899 and the firm celebrated its centenary with a £140m. turnover.

In August 1900 Coastguard Myles Mahoney rescued a boy who had fallen down the cliff at Beachy Head when on holiday.[1] This was the sixth such rescue in two years, and a three-page poem in the local newspaper ended with,

> Thank God for the hero spirit that lives where the British tread.
>
> Thank God for the brave hearts beating in the Coastguards of Beachy Head.

At the same time Trinity House was building the present Beachy Head lighthouse, for sadly the Belle Tout one had not proved satisfactory. While the light could be seen 23 miles out to sea on a clear night, in times of mist or fog, just when a poor sailor needed a bit of help, it was not visible at sea level.[2]

The present pier theatre opened on 15 July 1901. Apart from the 1,100-seat auditorium it contained offices, bars and tea-rooms, and at the apex was a camera obscura, the largest in the country at the time. Betty Palmer says, 'The camera obscura on the pier was remarkable. There was a large white disk, on which was focused views of Eastbourne. It could be turned to view most of the front and you could see people as far away as the Wish Tower as clear as clear.' A new bandstand was erected near the theatre, and halfway along two games saloons were added.

The foundation stone of Our Lady of Ransom Church in Grange Road was laid on 11 December 1900. Designed by F.A. Walters and built by Mark Martin in a late Gothic Decorated style of Bath stone, the church was opened on 15 December 1901 by Father Lynch in the presence of Bishop Bourne. It was not consecrated until 8 July 1926 because a Catholic church is not solemnly consecrated until all debt has been settled. It didn't stop a tower (1912), chancel and side chapels (1920), and recently a hall being added.

74 The Beachy Head lighthouse was built 1899-1902 and here it is nearing completion. The workmen, materials and equipment travelled down a cable from the top of the cliff to a work platform above the high water mark. This £20,814 replacement lighthouse was nearly 140ft. high, and built of five-ton Cornish granite blocks, all shaped at the quarry. The light came into operation on 2 October 1902, the Hood vaporiser being fuelled with a distillate similar to paraffin oil. The lighthouse was supplied with electricity in 1974 and automated in 1983. It shows two white flashes every 20 seconds, that can be seen 16 miles out to sea in almost all conditions.

75 Beachy Head *c*.1910. Eastbourne usually tops the sunshine league for mainland resorts and a great deal of Eastbourne's good weather can be attributed to the protection of Beachy Head. To the left is the *Beachy Head Hotel*, ahead are the coastguard cottages, and just to the right is the Watch Tower. Between 1877 and 1904 Lloyds of London had a signalman on Beachy Head to collect information of importance for the commodity and insurance markets about tea or wool clippers nearing the Thames. A message could be transmitted to London by semaphore in about 15 minutes, but ship telegraph made the system obsolescent. The Watch Tower became a postcard kiosk until 1939 (coinciding with the golden age of postcards from 1902) and is now an observation platform.

76   Eastbourne front, 1912. A peppery-looking 'Colonel' is pulled in a bathchair; his accompanying daughter looks like a 'thoroughly modern Miss' in slacks! The sunshades are everywhere, for only 'common' women allowed the sun on their face. The 'Birdcage' bandstand opened on 24 September 1894.

Private schools continued to be opened. One that flourishes in 2002 was started in 1894 by Mrs Anna Browne as a preparatory school for Eastbourne College. She called it St Bede's, after the Venerable Bede who had just been canonised. She sold it in 1901 to Mr G.H. Gowring, and St Bede's began its independent existence in Duke's Drive.

In 1898 Mr Freeman Freeman-Thomas MP of Ratton offered the Council 44 acres of wood and pasture around the duck decoy at a low price on condition it constructed a road from Eastbourne to Willingdon. The final offer of £3,000 for 82 acres was accepted and the road, which cost £10,277, is now King's Drive. Lord Rosebery opened Hampden Park on 12 August 1902 using a key embossed with the Eastbourne shield to unlock the gates. The park was named after the donor's grandfather, Viscount Hampden (Sir Henry Brand). It had mature oaks and a wildfowl lake, and 14 acres were earmarked as playing fields, with tennis courts, bowling and putting greens. Mr Freeman Freeman-Thomas was also landlord and first president of Willingdon Golf Club when it was extended to 18 holes in 1903. The clubhouse dates from 1904.

'The first live axle car we had seen' were Harry Caffyn's words when, in 1900, his electrical shop at 12 The Colonnade was asked to store a car. Further requests – no hotels had garages – convinced Percy Caffyn that the future lay in cars, although, as he pointed out, 'We didn't know what a garage

I paid a "surprise" visit
to the hospital at 9.30.
this morning – a found
anything in admirable
order – the wards being
specially well ventilated –

Edward R & I

July 13 - 1903.

G. L. Holford
Equerry in Waiting.

77 'I paid a "surprise" visit to the hospital at 9.30 this morning and found everything in admirable order – the wards being especially well ventilated. Edward RI July 13 1903.' The King maintained his support for the Princess Alice Hospital, and even donated an operating table on a visit in 1899. Queen Victoria did not come to the town and it is said this is why there are no statues of her, but Victoria Drive was opened in 1907.

78 By 1904 the Caffyn brothers' business had become Caffyn's Showrooms and Garage in Marine Parade.

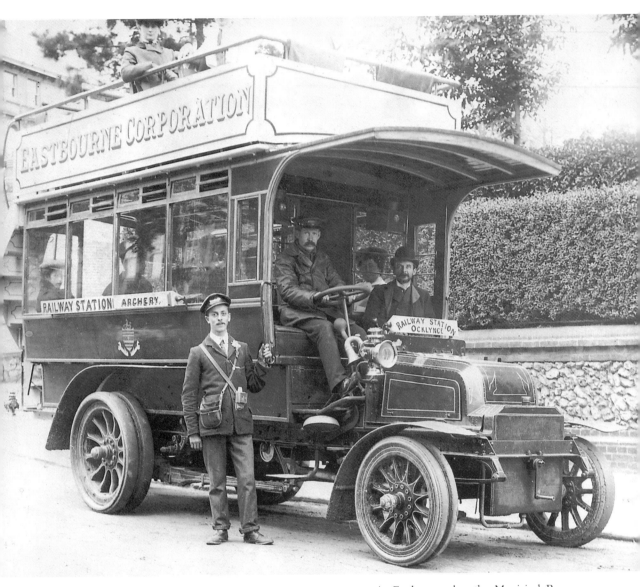

79 A 1904 Milnes-Daimler bus in Ocklynge. No trams were seen in Eastbourne, but the Municipal Bus Service, one of the earliest, commenced on 12 April 1903. A Motor Omnibus Depôt was built at Churchdale Road in 1911 at a cost of £3,947 and extended in 1922; it is now demolished. You could hail the bus at any point on its journey. Because of the road camber near the *Lamb Inn* on the Old Town route, passengers on the upper deck had to come downstairs in case the bus became top heavy and tilted over.

was, we called it a coach house.' Cars were first seen on Eastbourne's roads in May 1896, and the town's first motor taxi licence was issued to Mr H. Strudwick in 1899; the vehicle was restricted to certain routes and the speed was not to exceed 5m.p.h. within the Borough. Early registration letters were AP for Eastbourne and PN for East

Sussex. The first motor fatality occurred on 31 March 1904, when the little daughter of an Eastbourne builder was knocked down in Upperton Road, and the first car went over Beachy Head in 1908.

A chalk pit at the far western end of the Parades called Holywell was laid out as an Italian Garden

80 The entrance to the old Seaside library and public baths: the lending library was straight ahead, and the baths on the right, with separate days for men and women. You paid 3d. for a towel and soap, and entered a cubicle, each containing the bath, a chair, floor mat, a shelf and a hook for clothes. An attendant filled your bath (the taps were outside) and when it was to your liking he would leave. The cubicles were 'topless'. In 1982 the baths were taken over as rehearsal rooms by the EODS.

in 1904-5 to provide work for the unemployed. It cost all of £400, which the Council had to borrow.

Few houses in Seaside had bathrooms before the 1930s, and people couldn't afford Boot's 4d. library either. The opening on 28 July 1902 of the town's first purpose-built public library, and slipper baths, solved both problems at a cost of only £2,188. The popularity of the baths demanded more space, and after April 1924 they were extended, at a cost of £4,765, and the branch library moved along the road. The baths closed in 1976 and the premises

were bought for £35,000 by the Eastbourne Operatic and Dramatic Society. Richard Thornton, a great sportsman and mayor from 1911 to 1912, was a co-founder with Emeric Beaman of the EODS, which started in 1907 with a production of *Maritana* and celebrated its 75th Anniversary with *Kismet*, *The Merry Widow*, and *Hay Fever*.

Eastbourne badly needed a Central Library and a Technical College. In 1899 the Duke gave the land – the sites of the fire station, vestry hall and sheepwash in old Southbourne – and Andrew Carnegie, the US oil and steel millionaire and philanthropist, contributed the £10,000, so that the Duchess of Devonshire could open the Technical Institute on 8 August 1904. In May the next year Andrew Carnegie visited Eastbourne and was made a Freeman of the Borough. The ground floor was given over to the library and museum. The nucleus of the museum's antiquarian specimens had been collected by R.M. Caldecott of Meads Lodge (now Downs Court), Eastbourne's folly builder, but there was also a section on butterflies and moths, and the E.C. Arnold collection of birds, all shot and stuffed by the donor. The first floor held the Technical Institute and Continuation School, with the School of Art above.

Clement Brewer opened his Cavendish Place paint and wallpaper shop in 1904; it has spawned more than 100 branches all over the country. He mixed his paints on the premises from linseed oil, white lead and colours, and the womenfolk made up the flour and water paste.[3] Motcombe Swimming Baths in Old Town opened in January the next year, and Claude Achille Debussy, the French composer, escaped a scandal in Paris by staying at the *Grand Hotel* with his pregnant mistress. While there he completed *La Mer*.

The Queen Alexandra's Cottage Homes, in Seaside, opened on 5 June 1906 entirely free of debt, thanks to the mayor of the day, Cllr Charles Simmons. Intended for 'the ageing and deserving poor', the rent was 1d. a week. Queen Alexandra personally insisted on maximum fire-proofing. Three additional wings have been added over the years, and another was completed in the 1980s for the frailer residents. Princess Alexandra attended the Golden Jubilee.

At the junction of Meads Street with Meads Road stood the Links, built in 1869 and set in extensive

81 Officially opened in 1904, the Technical Institute and Library was a fine structure of red brick and Portland stone in a style similar to the Town Hall. In the early days borrowers chose their library book from a list and a member of staff hunted it out for them; only after 1911 were borrowers free to browse.

grounds. In 1901 Miss Hawtrey opened yet another Ladies' School here, which became famous under Miss Jane Potts between 1908 and 1925, drawing girls from the most fashionable circles. Miss Potts had been governess for 10 years to Princess Alice, Countess of Athlone (1883-1981), grand-daughter of Queen Victoria, who was devoted to her; her daughter, Lady May, became a pupil. Royal patronage assured the school of pupils such as Edwina Ashley (Lady Mountbatten), Dame Felicity Hyde Peake, later a Director of the WAAF, and Rachel Wrey, later Lady Willoughby de Brooke.[4]

The fashionable Royal Eastbourne Golf Club enlarged its course in 1904 and built a new clubhouse after the recently extended Paradise Road was cut through the old site.

Alfred Ryder, who ran a bookshop in South Street which he sold to Sidney Johnson in 1938, was at one time captain of the Eastbourne Downs Golf Club. He was barred from the Royal Eastbourne because he was in trade, but the Ryders did breach some barriers. Alfred's son, Thomas, won a scholarship to Eastbourne College, which lifted its 'ban' on the sons of tradesmen specifically for him. An outstanding sportsman, Thomas also won the MC in 1918. He became an accountant and his sons were pupils at St Cyprian's Prep School.

This famous school had started in 1900 in Carlisle Road, but moved to new buildings in Summerdown Road in 1906. The redoubtable headmaster and wife were Mr and Mrs Vaughan Wilkes, and it was Mrs Wilkes' presence that dominated the school.

82   The doctor, matron and nurses of the Isolation (later Downside) Hospital, East Dean Road, in 1902. This dated from 1885 and was extended in 1905. Miss M.G. Bailey was matron for 40 years. 'My brothers were taken away to the fever hospital with diphtheria, and men came and lit a sulphur candle to fumigate the attic bedroom where we all slept and no-one could enter for three days. I thought it was fun until I went down with it and was there for six weeks and had all my toys burnt.'

83   The Links, Meads, where Miss Potts, former royal governess, ran her school. The Countess of Athlone mentions that Miss Potts' hair was drawn into a bun, prompting the royal children to call her 'cowpat'. King Edward VII, however, always referred to Miss Potts as 'Mme Vase', or 'potty'. In the 1930s the Links became a holiday centre for the Methodist Guild. After war work as an Emergency Rest and Feeding Centre for bombed-out families, it thrived until 1998 when it was sold for development.

84   The pool at St Cyprian's School. The boys endured a Spartan regime with a pre-breakfast plunge whatever the weather. One old boy remarked, 'I spent four years in a German POW Camp, but my time at St Cyprian's had prepared me well.' In 1916 the school Classics prize was won by Eric Blair (George Orwell), the English prize by Cyril Connolly, the Arithmetic prize by Henry Longhurst, and the Drawing prize by Cecil Beaton.

There were about ninety boys with a dozen masters, a matron, carpenter, drill instructor, maids and gardeners. Mrs Wilkes taught English, Scripture and History (the school won the Harrow History Prize several years running) and encouraged 'simplicity, honesty and avoidance of verbiage', qualities evident in the writings of her pupils. Eric Blair (George Orwell) won two scholarships from the school, and it is reputed that his *Animal Farm* of 1945 was based on Willingdon. Other pupils included Reg Malden (Earl of Essex), Lord Mildmay, Gavin Maxwell, Nicholas Coldstream, Alan Clark (MP

and diarist) and a number of Cavendishes.[5] The school burnt down in May 1939, when one of the maids lost her life. It eventually moved to Oxford.

In 1884 the new Council established a Volunteer Fire Brigade, Eastbourne having been under East Sussex. J.A. Hounsom, a volunteer, became Chief Fire Officer in 1897, and a new fire station opened in Grove Road in 1905 at a cost of £6,250. The first motor fire engine was purchased in 1912 for £925, its water pump having a capacity of 400 gallons per minute and reach of 150 feet, but it had acetylene gas headlights. It was only considered

THE OLYMPIAN CONCERT PARTY. THE PIER. EASTBOURNE 1913.
HARRY KING.
HARRY JACKSON   ERNEST PITT   DOROTHY FALES   FRANKLYN VERNON   CHARLES HAWTHORNE

85 A Pierrot troupe, the Olympian Concert Party, performed on Eastbourne Pier in 1913.

surplus to requirements in 1937, but there was a proposal to reuse it in 1939. Not until Hounsom retired, in 1931, was the brigade reorganised, and D.W. Spence appointed its first professional Chief Officer.[6] The first fire engine to give the firemen protection from the elements was a £2,225 Dennis Limousine of 1936.

Eastbourne's third major golf course was constructed on Davies Gilbert land to the west of the town in 1907/8, following the success of the Royal and Willingdon clubs. Previously Eastbourne Artisans, it is now the Eastbourne Downs Club. As the course formed part of the Downs Purchase in 1926, the Borough Council remains the landlord. The original clubhouse on the hill is now a Youth Hostel, the present one being built in 1972.

About 1907 Tower Road, Tower Place and Tower Street, in Seaside, were renamed as Redoubt, St James and Latimer Roads, having developed an unsavoury reputation. With seven pubs, a beer house, and transient soldiery at the nearby Ordnance Yard, the area needed its own police station.

The many different private schools were an essential part of Eastbourne's economy, providing work for gardeners and maids, and buying everything from books to food in the town. Elise Randall would later say that she started her Eastbourne School of Domestic Economy in 1907 with one house, one girl and £5 in the bank. 'Ranny' was a character: she called everyone 'Darling', went everywhere on her bicycle, and was always throwing and going to parties. By 1939 the school was a prestigious place, and more hostels were bought; the students had to be in by 2200 hours.

Meads reached its zenith in Edwardian times. It remained until the Second World War an area of exclusive homes inhabited by the wealthy with servants to care for the grand mansions and gardens. Among the residents were a sprinkling of retired colonial administrators, military types, professionals and the self-made retired. Charles Rube made his fortune in South Africa, and among his houses was Ravenhurst in St John's Road. The largest monument in Ocklynge cemetery commemorates his son Ernest, an Army officer in India. The servants

86 After Bernard Fowler (1883-1967) married Josephine Oakley on 11 October 1913, they set off on their honeymoon in a car bought by her father. Fowler's EAC taught 19 men to fly before 1914, most of whom served in the war. Gustav Hamel (1889-1914) – of immortal fame – knew Eastbourne airfield well and looped-the-loop to delight the crowds, once in brilliant moonlight over the end of the pier. On landing he remarked that he had enjoyed seeing the lights of France.

got up at four in the morning to clear and polish the grates, and lay and light fires before the family came down. Time off was one evening a week and one day a month. Horses had to be groomed, their harness waxed, and their hooves polished black; with plaiting tails, feeding and cleaning out, the work was endless. George Meek, an Eastbourne bathchairman, wrote a book on his hard and un-rewarding work, with an introduction by H.G. Wells.[7]

Spencer Compton, 8th Duke of Devonshire, died in 1908. He left no legitimate children and was succeeded by a nephew, Victor Christian William, the 9th Duke (1868-1938). One of his tasks as mayor of Eastbourne from 1909 to 1910 was to proclaim the new King George V from the Town Hall balcony to a crowded Grove Road on 9 May 1910. Mark Martin, builder and developer, had preceded the Duke as mayor. It was the brickmaking activities of Mark Martin's firm that created the

Dallington Ponds. In the 1920s they were due to be filled in as required by the landowners, but were bought as a Bird Preserve. It is alleged that when Martin built Hampden Park Hall, as a present to the community, he used his broken and half bricks to keep the cost down.

The 9th Duke had death duties to find. He sold the Stud Farm at Jevington and again offered Devonshire Park to the Council for £110,665 and the Council accepted. Polls of electors in 1913 and 1914 were firmly against them running Sunday concerts and holding a licence for intoxicating liquors.

Moving pictures were allowed. A film had been shown on the pier in 1903, but the first public show was in the Constitutional Club's building. When the New Picture Hall opened, it became the Tivoli Cinema.[8] In 1912 the Seaside Road cinema had 'Performances daily at 3, 7 and 9pm. Reserved seats 1s. and unreserved 6d., 4d., 3d.' By this time the Tivoli had been joined by the

87   A Cabmen's Shelter on the front erected about 1900. It so impressed the King of Spain, who was staying at the *Grand Hotel*, that he had an identical one built in Madrid. It was destroyed in the Spanish Civil War.

Eastern Cinema in Seaside, the Electric Theatre in Seaside Road, later the Central, and the Kinemacolor in the Devonshire Pavilion. Apart from between 1940 and 1944, the Tivoli entertained Eastbourne residents and visitors until its final closure in 1982.

Blériot's monoplane was on display at the Devonshire Park a mere nine days after the epic channel crossing in July 1909. On 19 April 1911 a plane (crash)landed in the Park. In that year the census population was 52,542, and the town was incorporated as a County Borough on 1 April. It was largely thanks to the initiative and drive of Frederick Bernard Fowler, who taught himself to fly a Blériot monoplane, that the town acquired the Eastbourne Aviation Company (EAC) and its own airfield. Established in December 1911, it

was just west of St Anthony's; a seaplane base followed at the Crumbles end of Lottbridge Drove.[9]

With 2,158 hours of sun in 1911, tourism was boosted. New suites had been built on the west wing of the *Grand Hotel*, and the chairman of the Grand Hotel Company reported that champagne was a necessity so several hundred pounds worth of vintage were tucked away in the cellars. Full board was 12s. 4d. a day, so the hotel porters came in livery with white wigs, knee breeches and silk stockings for their £1 a week.

The Joe Vine who took part with Frank Woolley in the record seventh wicket stand of 143 during the 1911/12 tour of Australia was a local man. Joe started his cricket on Lord Willingdon's ground and played for Sussex and England.

The first X-rays at the Princess Alice Hospital were taken in 1912, the year the original pier entrance kiosks of the 1870s were replaced by a set of larger ones, which lasted until 1951. Eastbourne was shaken to its foundations when, in October that year, Police Inspector A. Walls was murdered.[10] The coachman of a brougham had seen a man on a canopy above the door of 6 South Cliff Avenue and informed the police. At 1940 hours Walls, the seafront inspector and a year from retirement, went up to the man saying, 'Come down old chap, do,' whereupon the burglar lent down and shot Walls, who staggered into the roadway where he died. The burglar went under many aliases, John Williams being the one on the charge sheet. Florence, his moll, who called him George Seymour, and John MacKie, his brother, were part of a criminal set. After the shooting, Williams and Flo went to the Picture Palace to see *Dante's Inferno*! Thousands attended the Inspector's funeral on 16 October, while Williams was tried, found guilty, and hanged the next year.

Similar publicity was given to the death of a musician who had played in all the local orchestras. His memorial, now in a Central Bandstand shelter, was unveiled on 24 October 1914 by Clara Butt. It shows a portrait of the musician, the sinking *Titanic*, and an inscription: '... erected as a tribute to John Wesley Woodward ... who, with ... the ship's band perished ... through the sinking of the ... Titanic on April 15th 1912.'

Eastbourne's inaugural meeting of the Women's Social and Political Union was in 1913, and on 8 April that year phosphorus was posted in local pillar boxes. There was outrage in the town when in May hassocks were set on fire at St Anne's Church and 'Votes, Votes, Votes' scratched on a religious painting. In April 1914 a Felixstowe hotel was torched by two suffragettes, one of whom was Miss Florence Tunks of Eastbourne. The town's record of suffragette action was lost with St Anne's in the Second World War, along with a brass to the memory of a parishioner, Captain Lawrence Oates, who walked out to his death in an Antarctic snowstorm rather than delay Captain Falcon Scott and his comrades.

The laying of the foundation stone of St Aidan's Methodist Church, Seaside was in 1913. The vicar

88 Rupert Chawner Brooke (1887-1915), poet and icon of his age, made several visits to Eastbourne and stayed at the *Beachy Head Hotel* in 1911. Like so many of his generation, Brooke was to die in the war, in his case from an infected insect bite on his way to the Dardanelles. George Bernard Shaw (1856-1950) is said to have learnt to bicycle at Eastbourne, and Mabel Lucie Attwell (1879-1964), artist and writer, known for her caricatures of children, lived at Ocklynge Manor, Mill Road into the 1930s.

was from St Aidan's in Northumberland. The organ was pumped by hand for the first 34 years. The walls of the church bulged because it was built on beach and it was demolished for sheltered housing in 2002.

The funeral of Carew Davies Gilbert in December that year was in an overflowing St Mary's Church. He was 61, old for the time, and had been lord of the manor of Eastbourne during the town's most rapid development. He donated the Seaside Recreation Ground on the occasion of Queen

89 Louis G. Ford made his first sale at his ironmongery shop on newly built Station Parade in January 1912, alongside coal merchants Rickett's and Bradford's, who had been there some time in one-storey huts. Ford later extended to Wharf Road and along both sides of Terminus Road. That year the Post Office was built opposite, at 3 Upperton Road, and Bobby & Co. Ltd (now Debenham's) completed their department store.

Victoria's Golden Jubilee in 1887, the Gilbert Recreation Ground (now Prince's Park), and the land for St Anne's Church. Interment took place at East Dean, the coffin carried on a farm wagon from Eastbourne with eight bearers walking alongside dressed in smocks.

On 22 December 1,000 poor children marched to the Floral Hall at Devonshire Park for their Christmas treat. They were greeted by their host, Charles Jewell, and sat down to a meal of a buttered Scotch pancake, a sausage roll, a quarter pound of Genoa cake and a bun, with milk and tea to drink. After entertainment, each child left with a bag containing a Christmas cracker, a bar of chocolate, two apples and a banana. Mr. Jewell was a philanthropist who, having made his money in Argentine cattle ranches, retired to Silverdale

Road, complaining of income tax at 2½ per cent. He raised funds for the Soldiers' and Sailors' Home in Upperton Road, started by Flora McCartie in 1905 to teach disabled ex-servicemen a trade.

When a squadron of the Home Fleet visited, in July 1914, 15,000 people passed through the pier turnstiles, paying £294. The Sussex County Agricultural Show was also held that month on fields near Summerdown Road soon to be put to other uses. At the end of the month Eastbourne's Tuberculosis Hospital opened at a cost of £2,143, plus £1,250 to the Davies Gilberts for the site. It was built at the edge of the town because TB was the 'plague' of the age: of the first 1,000 patients 530 died. A typical account read, 'In 1927 my mother became tired and the doctor said it was consumption. She was sent to the Gildredge TB

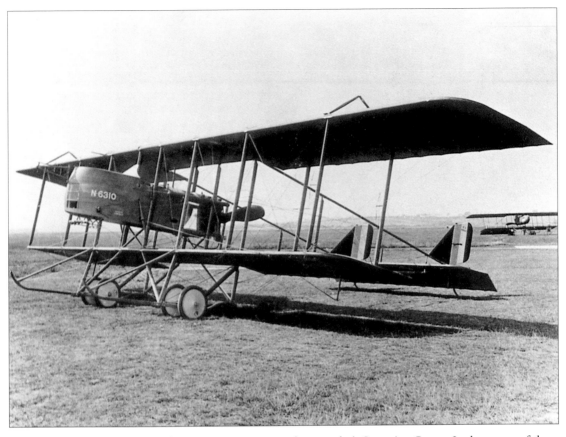

90 A factory to build planes for war service was erected near today's Sovereign Centre. In the course of the war 252 aircraft were assembled in the EAC sheds on the Crumbles. This is an EAC-built Maurice Farman pusher biplane of July 1917.

Hospital, now demolished for Bodmin Close, but died the next year aged 42.'

Arthur Clarkson Rose, who worked with Olive Fox, appeared at Seaford over the summer of 1914 in his first concert party. During the next 50 years there was seldom a Christmas without him in pantomime, or a summer without a production of *Twinkle*, but otherwise after 4 August 1914 life was never the same. Stewart Thorpe recalls, 'On August Bank Holiday I heard my father speaking of the invasion of Belgium. A few weeks later a column of Lancashire Fusiliers halted in Junction Road while their officer knocked on doors to billet the men, and the house owners had to take them. The Fusiliers drilled in Devonshire Place and off duty they sat on the pavement playing cards, usually Brag. Very

shocking to genteel Eastbourne, but they were cut to pieces in France.'

Eastbourne's airfield was requisitioned by the Admiralty as a Royal Naval Air Service base to train pilots, and 118 British, Canadian, American, Brazilian and Japanese pilots qualified there. Flying was a dangerous game and 21 trainees lost their lives in accidents. The airfield became the home of 206 and 50 Training Depôt Squadrons, and at its closure it extended over 242 acres, had 32 buildings, and housed 76 planes and 839 personnel.

A small military hospital had existed at the Ordnance Yard, Seaside during most of 19th century, but given the casualties in France it became clear that more hospitals were needed. In October 1914 the Red Cross opened Urmston, in Granville Road, the Soldiers' and Sailors' Home, and Wish

91 Upperton, at 9 Upperton Road, was one of the houses taken over by the Red Cross for a hospital in the First World War. It had 70 beds in two-bedded wards named after war heroes and heroines such as Cavell, Beatty and Jellicoe. The Medical Officers gave their services free, there were two paid nurses, and the rest were volunteers. Although they weren't the most seriously wounded, only one patient died from 1,400. This photograph was taken after Upperton became the Maternity Home in 1920. It has since been demolished for Marlborough Court.

Rocks, but the latter two were replaced by Upperton and de Walden Court. Kempston opened in March 1915, and Fairfield Court in October 1915. The last, Redburn, opened in April 1916. All had closed by December 1918. Trains bringing the casualties were met by volunteers who moved them to the hospitals by bus or cars. Usually, one train a month brought in about 150 cases, but at the time of the Somme in 1916 there was one a week. After the war Redburn became Chelmsford Hall School.[11]

Eastbourne was a training centre for RAMC recruits, first at Whitbread Hollow (Beachy Head) and later Summerdown Road. Roland Burke, the Duke's agent, was Clerk of Works and the Royal Engineers built wooden huts on brick bases to hold 3,500 in total. The camp offered rehabilitation, good food, and entertainment, 'varying from a dental clinic to a skittle alley'. The 'Blue-Boys' wore a light-blue jacket and trousers, white shirt and red

tie, so they were readily seen, especially by the Military Police. Despite a changing complement the camp ran a famous concert party, Knuts Kamp Komedy Kompany. It was alleged that if you were good enough to get in you enjoyed a far longer convalescence than was medically required. Even so, over 90 per cent returned to active service.

The YMCA provided accommodation for servicemen's relatives at their Union Jack Club, Windsor Terrace, and Charles Jewell did his bit, buying the premises in order to keep the property in good repair. They are currently occupied by a youth club called 'Charlies'.

Lieutenant Cyril Gordon Martin DSO, whose family lived in Grange Road, won a V.C. near Ypres on 12 March 1915. He held off a German counter attack for over two hours although he was wounded. At home there was a shell shortage scandal. Eastbourne's Bus Depôt offered their services and, before the Armistice, produced 370,000 mortar

92 Summerdown Camp, looking towards Upland Road. The camp was bounded by Summerdown Road on the east, Paradise Drive to the south, the golf course, and Pashley Road, which only had two houses in 1915, to the north. The main road through the camp became Old Camp Road. The first convalescents arrived in April 1915, and before February 1920 almost 150,000 troops passed through what was probably the largest camp of its kind in Europe. The troops had film shows on Sundays, which was not allowed in the town.

bombs as well as assembling mines. The total value was £203,000 and a profit of £25,900 was divided between the Corporation and the staff. Eastbourne College and Caffyn's and Lovely's Garages also made shell cases or assembled aircraft.

To meet Lord Kitchener's appeal for 100,000 volunteers, Colonel Lowther of Herstmonceux Castle aimed to raise a local battalion for the Royal Sussex Regiment, and enough men for three battalions volunteered; they were known as Lowther's Lambs because of their mascot. Their medical examination was by a doctor, who was paid a shilling, but only for every man he passed fit. The Lambs went to France in 1916. On 30 June they were in action for four hours. No ground was gained but 350 were killed and 1,000 wounded, about half the strength. CSM Nelson Victor Carter, of Greys Road, born in Eastbourne in 1887, won a posthumous V.C. that day. He captured a German machine-gun post and turned

it on the enemy, but was killed bringing in wounded.

Next it was the turn of the workhouse to contribute to the war effort. The inmates were moved out and the buildings converted into the Eastbourne Central Military Hospital. This was for critically ill patients, the first of whom was admitted in January 1916. At its height there were 300 patients here, eight nursing sisters, 44 male nurses, and 25 VADs. In all 16,000 were treated before closure in July 1919, and 100 deaths occurred, two being of nurses from influenza.

The Cavalry Command Depôt was opened to bring healthy men up to the standard of fitness required for front line duty. It was sited on Corporation land, bought in 1913 for building affordable houses and now bounded by Beechy Avenue, Victoria Gardens and Victoria Drive. It also had a band and a concert party, one of the star performers being a certain Sgt. George Robey. It closed at the end of the war, although its service to Eastbourne wasn't ended. The 16th Canadian Base Hospital opened at All Saints in January 1917, mainly for Seaford units; fully equipped, it had a pharmacy, X-ray, laboratories and a cinema. Later in 1917 a Catholic order of nuns opened Fernbank, in Hartington Place, for wounded officers. It became Esperance, a private nursing home.

Jack Warne wrote,

> The war had not affected Eastbourne. Holidaymakers came as in peacetime, the *Grand Hotel*'s receipts and profits rocketed, and the wounded soldiers at Summerdown Camp, and in the big houses converted into hospitals, were a tonic to the town. The 'Blue Boys' were a happy lot and they put on shows, such as pantomimes, sports days and galas, and I never associated them with the grim struggle in France. Until one day in 1917 when I saw people near the pier. The word bandied round was 'survivors' and shortly a group of sailors, bareheaded, barefooted in bedraggled blue uniforms, came past the kiosks. They looked strained and exhausted and the crowd saw them pass in silence. It emerged that they were from HMS *Ariadne,* an 11,000-ton minelayer, sunk six miles out by U-65, with the loss of 33 lives.

Over 50 ships were sunk by U-boats off Eastbourne and Beachy Head, from 23 February 1915, when the collier *Branksome Chine* was sunk by U-8, to the last recorded sinking, the trooper SS *Moldavia,* torpedoed in 1918 by U-57. Fifty-six lives were lost, but they were almost the only casualties of two million Americans carried across the Channel. Rationing meant residents needed no encouragement to work the allotments provided by the Corporation and Compton Estate. By 1917 there were appeals for an end to the heavy eating of the Edwardian era; 'people with more money than decency were indulging their appetites'.[12] Another sign of the times was the town's first venereal diseases clinic. It was discreetly housed in a hut at the rear of the Town Hall, after the Princess Alice and the Leaf hospitals refused to provide a service, afraid that donors would desert them.

The Polegate Airship Station operated antisubmarine patrols from its 1,442-acre site around Coppice Avenue and Broad Road. Losses were rare, the worst being the disaster of 20 December 1917, when a mist came up over the base station with five airships airborne. They all landed safely at temporary moorings, but after a wind got up two airships on Beachy Head moved off and aimed for Polegate. SSZ19 reached the base safely, but SSZ7 drifted towards Jevington and landed on SSZ10 moored there. Both airships were burnt out, but two of the three crew were saved by RNAS mechanics, who were awarded the Albert (George) Medal.

Grand Parade was associated once more with scandalous wrongdoings when George Hayes, lodged at 22 Grand Parade, was called up for the Forces in 1918. He attempted to buy the birth certificate of another George Hayes, aged 51, and was reported to the police. At his trial in May he was found guilty, but Major Edward Teale, the Chief Constable of Eastbourne, spoke for him at the trial and his sentence was only three months. The uproar was such that an enquiry into the Chief Constable's conduct was instituted and it became clear there had been an improper attempt to influence the court. Major Teale resigned in July, but subsequently claimed his pension on the grounds of ill health.

The Armistice was greeted with thanksgiving and jubilation, and with dancing on the Western Lawns. By May 1919 all the women employed to replace men had been discharged, and there were those who thought that the old ways would return. For quite a few families there would be a permanent change: Ocklynge cemetery has 130 war graves, and there are others in Langney cemetery. J. Andrews Ltd of Willingdon Road and Francis & Sons of Junction Road made the standard headstones for Eastbourne. Those buried locally had a funeral with full military honours, the ceremonies ranging from a few relatives to civic occasions; for that of Lt. Col. Oswald Fitzgerald, Lord Kitchener's ADC, who drowned with his chief and whose family lived in Carlisle Road, over 2,000 lined the route.

Many survivors were scarred by their experiences. An organ grinder who stood on the front, bowlerhatted and wearing medal ribbons as he churned out 'Let's All Go Down the Strand' and 'Daisy, Daisy', turned the handle with one arm, the other an empty pinned-up sleeve. The first hint of more trouble ahead was a report in the *Eastbourne Gazette* of 10 July 1918 that three huts had been closed at Summerdown Camp because of influenza. In

October schools were closed, and by March the next year 180 persons, aged from 15 to 35, had died in the town from the flu pandemic.[13] Of the 191 Canadian graves in Seaford cemetery, 114 were almost certainly influenza victims, 70 of whom died at All Saints' Hospital.

Thousands watched on 10 November 1920 as General Lord Horne unveiled Eastbourne's War Memorial to the one in fifty residents who died in the war. Canon W. Streatfeild conducted a short memorial service, and Sir Charles Harding, the deputy mayor but mayor through the war, referred to Eastbourne's contributions.[14] The names of the fallen are carved on oaken tablets in the Town Hall. In recognition of Eastbourne's record War Bonds sales, a 26-ton tank was presented to the town. It rusted away at Gildredge Park and went for scrap just about the time the next war began.

The Eastbourne branch of the League of Nations Union was formed in November 1919 with Dr Henry Farnell as chairman. The branch had a tolerant and realistic attitude and was supported by both pacifists and communists, and when the United Nations was established in 1945 it simply changed its name. The Rev. Dr James Reid, Percy Caffyn, the Rev. Geoffrey Bellhouse and his wife

93 Fragment of fabric from an aircraft showing that it had been assembled by Caffyn's of Eastbourne.

Lucy all enthusiastically promoted the ideals of the UN.

The Ordnance Yard Hospital in Seaside closed after 1918, and the years just after the war were marked by auctions of items left in the various camps, from complete huts to pillowcases. In 1919

94 The Central Military Hospital in 1917, when it successfully treated the two survivors of the Polegate airship tragedy. The staff are in front of the ex-workhouse building. King George V and Queen Mary visited Eastbourne on 3 May 1916 and toured the hospital. Nurse E.E. Bumstead said, 'There was great excitement. They were accompanied by the Prince of Wales and Princess Mary, both in uniform, the Princess looking so much the "English Rose" with her lovely complexion.'

the Council purchased the huts at the Command Depôt for use as temporary housing, the first families moving in that summer. These 'homes for heroes' had no insulation, the only water taps and lavatories were outside, and they were noisy, damp, and cold. Mrs Sally Sands' father had been a patient in the Central Military Hospital, having been gassed, and her parents started married life in The Hutments: 'He developed TB and died at 40.'

The peak year for occupation was 1923, with 600 residents, but gradually the Council replaced the huts and by 1932 all that was left were the street names: Command Road and Cavalry Crescent. In 1920 the Council opened six huts as an open air school, at a time when childhood rickets and TB were common; the huts were not replaced by brick pavilions until the 1930s. It became the Downs School in 1959 and continues to teach children with learning difficulties.

The 1920/1 football season was most successful for the Eastbourne Royal Engineers Old Comrades, formed in 1894 as the Sussex Royal Engineers, and Eastbourne United from 1952. They won the East Sussex Cup, beating the Royal Corps of Signals in the final, when the first radio transmission of a sporting event was made from Eastbourne. In 1946 the Council helped the club move to the Princes Park Oval where, under the chairmanship of Alderman Percy Wood, they raised funds to build a grandstand. The Eastbourne Men's Hockey Club was founded in 1919, though there are references to men's hockey at Larkin's Field before 1900. Many girls' schools also played in the 1890s, about the time the Hockey Association was formed, but the women's club wasn't formed until 1950.

The Duke's Orchestra was merged with the Council's Municipal Orchestra, and Captain Henry Amers became conductor of the 35-piece Devonshire Park Orchestra, with a contract to provide a military band. This was the start of a fine record of orchestral and military band concerts, which continues. Captain Amers was Eastbourne's Director of Music from 1920 to 1936. From 1924 he conducted a Municipal Orchestra at the Winter Garden which, with a strength of 40, was the largest such orchestra in the country. Always impeccably dressed, in a military style with belt and sash, Amers was an able and popular musician; he had such a

trim figure it was whispered he wore a corset! In 1923 Captain Amers inaugurated an Annual Musical Festival. Some performances were broadcast, and Eric Coates and Sir Edward Elgar were among the favourite conductors. For more popular tastes, as Gordon Brown recalls, 'It was the age of jazz, and dancing was all the rage. My sister was at Hillcote School, and would insist on being taken to the Winter Garden *thé dansant* for Jenkie's Band. There was Miss Jenkinson at the piano and Captain Street on drums. He had lost a leg in the war.' The story behind Captain Street shooting himself on the Brighton train remains untold.

Gordon Brown was at Aldro, a prep school of some 55 boys in Darley Road, Meads, now part of the Brighton University campus. Boys at the school included many Bentalls, Sainsburys and Pertwees. Geoffrey Hallowes, who married Odette, the French resistance heroine, was another, and Kim Philby, the master spy who changed masters, was head boy in 1924.

The Rev. Edwin Browne bought the school housed in Colstocks farmhouse and turned it into a successful preparatory school, St Andrew's. Three of his brothers, Harold, Lionel and Charles, also taught at the school, and after Edwin's death in 1933 Harold's son, Francis, became joint head-master.

Eversley Court, 14 St Anne's Road, which had been Ascham School from 1893 but was taken over by the RNAS during the war, was bought by the County Borough for £13,733 in 1919 to house Eastbourne Grammar School for Boys. The following year the Municipal Girls' Secondary School moved into 5 Upperton Road, and its junior departments next door at The Glen, both large detached houses dating from the 1860s.

At the instigation of Dr W.G. Willoughby, the Borough purchased the next house, the old Red Cross Hospital at 9 Upperton Road, for £4,179 from the Davies Gilbert family. Dr Willoughby was the Medical Officer of Health from 1894 to 1939 and a Freeman of the Borough. Willoughby Crescent, Seaside, is named after him. In 1920 the hospital opened as a Maternity Home, for married mothers only. With extensions it provided 25 beds, and over 20,000 babies were born there before closure in 1976. Mothers paid two guineas a week

95   Unveiling of the War Memorial in November 1920. The 6ft. bronze statue on a 10ft. high granite pedestal represents the Angel of Peace and Victory and was sculpted by H.C. Fehr. It was on the site of the Princess Alice Tree, at the junction of Devonshire Place, South Street, Cornfield Road and Bolton Road.

and stayed on average 17½ days, enjoying the rest. Before 1918 there were no district midwives, but each doctor who practised obstetrics had a 'handy woman', some handier than others.

By 1921 Chapman's bus firm was offering three tours a season to the Flanders battlefields. The organisation required was considerable, for the vehicles had little luggage capacity and were so unreliable that a back-up vehicle was often used to carry petrol, spares and luggage.

There were two grisly murders on the Crumbles around this time. The first, labelled 'The Séance on the Shingle', was a sad little story. Irene Munro, 17, came to Eastbourne for her holidays and on 19 August 1920 labourers working on the Crumbles Ballast Line saw her 'happy and laughing in the company of two men'. Later that day another holidaymaker found a woman's foot sticking out of the shingle near the line. The body was that of Irene and a nearby piece of stone had been used to

96 The Knapp family bought the guardroom hut of the Command Depôt after the war and opened it as The Bungalow Stores, in Victoria Drive. It provided a needy service for The Hutments and in 1927 the business was transferred over the road to newly built Albert Parade.

batter her to death. Descriptions of the two men were obtained from the workmen, and Jack Field, 19, and William Gray, 28, both unemployed, were apprehended on the seafront. There was little doubt of their guilt, although each claimed the other had struck the fatal blow, and both were executed the next year.

Sir Bernard Spilsbury, the renowned forensic pathologist, declared that the second Crumbles murder, of 1924, was his most interesting case.[15] Patrick Mahon, 34, was good-looking, dressed well, spoke fluent French, had a good position and salary as a sales manager, but was a persistent philanderer with a record of embezzlement and violent robbery. Emily Kaye, 37, fell for him and struck up a relationship though she knew he was married. She found herself pregnant, and told her friends she was going away with 'Pat'. Scotland Yard, having been tipped off, arrested Mahon when he collected

a bag at Waterloo Station and he admitted that Emily had been to Eastbourne with him.

On the Crumbles was a row of coastguard cottages, now gone, and Mahon had rented one. Inside was found a trunk, with the initials EBK, which held human body parts, and saucepans with particles of human flesh. Spilsbury reassembled the pieces and showed that the parts were of a pregnant woman, but the skull was missing and he could not say how she died. Spilsbury said to proceed, but a good case could not be made against Mahon.

At his trial Mahon, however, convicted himself. Spilsbury showed that death in the manner described by Mahon was not possible, and the police found that a knife Mahon claimed he bought after the death had been bought beforehand. Found guilty, he was hanged at Wandsworth.

To provide work for the unemployed the Council erected a wooden tea chalet and shelter on the promenade below the Holywell Italian Gardens at a cost of £912. A brick-built café later replaced the chalet. Unemployed men were also used to lay out gardens at the Redoubt, Gildredge Hospital, and the Archery and Gilbert Recreation Grounds.

The EAC went to the wall. Some buildings were sold in 1924 to Eastbourne Corporation to store deck chairs in the winter, and the large steel hanger, bought by Wenham's as a furniture repository, lasted until the 1987 'hurricane'. The Post Office, on the other hand, which had taken over the National Telephone Co. in 1911, was expanding, and in 1923 the local exchange transferred to the HPO in Upperton Road. 'The Post Office was run on military lines, the postmen saluted Major Headley, the Postmaster, who inspected every one before they went on their rounds', according to Douglas Swift, a Post Office messenger boy.

John Chisholm Towner was an auctioneer, estate agent and Council member who, in 1919, left a bequest of £6,000 and his collection of pictures to the County Borough to form an art gallery. Two years later the Borough bought for £19,000 the Manor House and grounds in Borough Lane vacated by the Davies Gilbert family. The Towner Art Gallery and Manor Gardens opened in 1923, with Arthur F. Reeve-Fowkes, Director of Art at the Technical Institute, as the curator until 1947. The Towner was visited by Queen Mary in 1935. Gildredge Park and Manor Gardens between them had hard and grass tennis courts and included herbaceous borders, a pond, extensive lawns and many established trees; an aviary was a feature for some years. The grounds have a hermitage of c.1790, recently restored.

In 1924 the Redoubt was finally sold to the Corporation by the Army Council for £150, and opened to the public, the land adjoining the Redoubt having been offloaded by the Duke in 1905. To the west of the Redoubt it was laid out as a music garden around a bandstand and, later, a sun lounge was added where refreshments were available. To the east, stretching to Princes Park, were two bowling greens, an 18-hole putting green and tennis courts.

In the 1920s there were three types of bather: those who used a Corporation bathing cabin to undress and store their clothes (at 6d. for 30 min-

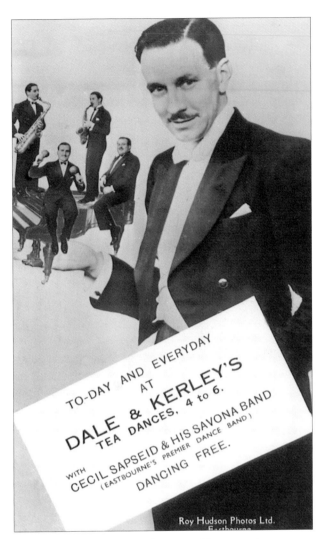

97 The 'twenties were the Age of Jazz even in Eastbourne: 'The thrill of dancing to the music of Cecil Sapseid's band! The heart-ache when the end of a perfect evening was signalled by the strains of his signature tune, "Good Night Sweetheart", seemed unbearable.'

utes); those who changed in the canvas enclosures, separate for men and women, at each end of the promenade (1d. a time); and the terrible 'Mackintosh bathers'. These individuals ran from their house or hotel, swam, and rushed back in a wet costume. Such behaviour, even before 8a.m., could barely be condoned.

By now bathing was popular along the whole of the front and at Birling Gap. Sea bathing at

98　Curious folk peering over the wall of the old coastguard officer's cottage where Emily Beilby Kaye was murdered in 1924.

Eastbourne is particularly safe with the gentle slope of the foreshore, although at high tide the sloping shingle beaches mean that bathers can be out of their depth just a few steps out.

In the 1920s the Dobie family ran 22 Grand Parade as an apartment house. They lived in the basement in summer and rented the floors above to guests who booked from year to year, took a whole floor and brought their servants. Among the regulars were the Rajah and Ranee of Sarawak, General Lord French, and Mr Tanley of Tansad furniture. The Dobies sold to the *Burlington Hotel* in 1929 and the ground floor became Bertie's Bar, and Marks & Spencer moved into their present shop. The new Ministry of Health declared that workhouses were to be renamed 'Institutions' and, with the appointment of Miss Mary Letheren in 1924, the building of new wards and the abolition of the Guardians in 1930, the infirmary could be renamed St Mary's Hospital, and new standards set. With Dr Herbert MacAleenan as the medical superintendent,

Matron Letheren rolled up her sleeves and turned the place into a well-loved hospital, helping all Eastbourne.

Hampden Park now had a well-matured look, and was surrounded by a high fence and locked gates at night. Henty, the park keeper, dressed in the same serge uniform summer and winter: 'Wot keeps out the winter cold keeps out the summer 'eat.' Other characters included a lady who would hire a cart to distribute birdseed, at some discomfort to cyclists, a man who walked around with a sticker on his hat saying 'Beware of Lawyers', and the kleptomaniac welcomed by shopkeepers: he went into shops, filled his pockets and walked out, only for his accompanying manservant to pay whatever the shopkeeper suggested.

Between the wars Admiral Sir Robert Prendergast was owner of part of de Walden Lodge. He had an extra horn installed in the back of his Rolls-Royce so that he could honk at other drivers to the embarrassment of his chauffeur. William

99   Hampden Park and its pond in 1922. Created by damming a stream, it had been part of the Ratton Estate duck decoy, which consisted of three narrowing tubes of netting down which the ducks flew, to be trapped and killed for sale. Hence the name of nearby Decoy Drive.

Gratwicke Heasman, big game hunter and sportsman, lived at Michelgrove. He played cricket for Sussex from 1885 to 1895, and K.S. Duleepsinhji lodged with him. He took a morning swim for many years, and never had a car; he 'preferred dogs and horses to modern day fangles'. In 1914, the year the Meads Road entrance of the Saffrons Sports Ground was built, he was the first to ask Maurice Tate to open an innings. Heasman was surely at the ground when Archie MacLaren's team of amateurs soundly beat Warwick Armstrong's all-conquering 1921 Australian XI.[16] Reginald Summerhays established the Eastbourne Riding School in the 1920s, and was one of the first in the country to offer riding opportunities to those who did not own a horse.

Between the wars long queues were seen every Friday and Saturday night for admission to cinemas, which included the Classic (Trinity Place, now flats), Elysium, Gaiety (Seaside), Luxor (Pevensey Road, later *ABC*), Mansells New Central, New Eastern (Old Town) and Plaza (High Street). There was also a News Theatre near where the Co-op is now. 'We paid 4d. at the Picturedrome in Langney Road (later the Curzon), all black and white and silent, except for the mood-inducing pianist; we fell about at the antics of Charlie Chaplin and Harold Lloyd, but the cowboy films were our favourites. When we came out it was such an anticlimax, back to ordinary people and things. If you felt rich you went to the New Gallery Kinema in Terminus Road, but it cost 6d. and needed careful consideration. For 3d. the Regent in Old Town had comedy films and cartoons; it was a mad house, all the children yelling and shouting, and we came out deafened, but it was great fun.' The popularity of 'the pictures' was responsible for Astaire Avenue, named after Adele Astaire, the film star dancer's sister, who in 1932 married Lord Charles Cavendish.[17]

The old habits hadn't gone completely. In the 1920s, when any decent house had one, there were

100 Charles Montagu Doughty (1843-1926), the Arabian traveller and writer, author of the prose classic *Travels in Arabia Deserta*, lived in the town from 1906 to his death. He received Prince Feisal of Iraq at 18 Southfields Road in the 1920s. On occasions a Brough Superior motor bike would have been propped up outside, for another visitor was J.H. Ross, alias T.E. Shaw and better known as Lawrence of Arabia (1888-1935).

four shops selling pianos in the centre of East-bourne. Mind you, by the 1950s you couldn't give them away: when Canon Denys Giddey, hospital chaplain, appealed for a piano in 1961, not only was he offered enough to fill a ward, but two were dumped without notice on the hospital steps. The shops have gone too. S. Hermitage & Sons' music emporium was there until the war, and Lindridges, its grand pianos and musical instruments surrounded by palm trees and the busts of composers, lasted only a few years more; it's now Superdrug.

Eastbourne started to tarmac its streets in 1911, and by the 1930s the water carts used to lay the

dust had gone, although you can still see the topping-up points in the town. The Duke again offered Devonshire Park in 1923 and again met ratepayer opposition. The next year, however, the lots were put on the market and the Borough acquired the Devonshire Baths and manager's house for £16,500. The Council added £10,000 Turkish Baths and, in 1930, £5,000 was spent on new heating. The next year new toilets were installed and the tiling was changed, and a further £2,500 went on a new filtration plant; the expenditure was worthwhile for the baths were in heavy use in the 1930s after mixed bathing came in.

Alice Hudson became Eastbourne's first woman mayor in 1926. During the General Strike of that year all the bus drivers came out, but the service was run by volunteers. About this time a battle was being waged against speculative building on the Beachy Head Downs. Only the endeavours of Arthur Beckett and the Society of Sussex Downsmen, with help from W.C. Campbell, H. Hornby Lewis, Rudyard Kipling and others, ensured that the £17,000 required to buy the land was raised, and the Seven Sisters was presented to the National Trust. Eastbourne Council decided in 1926 to purchase an area of 4,100 acres of Downland on Beachy Head, the aim being to keep it as open space in perpetuity for all to enjoy.[18] It was finally bought in 1929 for £91,291.

The YMCA Annual Conference was first held at Eastbourne in March 1928. The conference trade was to extend the tourist season and even supplant some of the holiday trade, and Rotary International, who first came in October 1931, continues to choose Eastbourne. The Eastbourne Round Table (number 32) was formed that year, with Dr Bodkin Adams as one of the founder members. The *Grand Hotel* was doing well. It had its own farm, its visitors' book read like an international Debrett, and from 1924 to 1939 and for some time after 1945 it provided the BBC with its earliest long-running success as the Palm Court Orchestra charmed listeners. Mrs Jack Byfield remembers, 'The elegant lounge was decorated in the palest green and gold, enhanced by a plum-coloured carpet and a unique French chandelier above. The orchestra included "the man with the singing violin", Albert Sandler, leader 1924-8, Henry Cousden was second violin, Jack

101   The Commemorative Seat on Beachy Head, to mark the Downs' purchase, was unveiled by the Duke and Duchess of York (later King George VI and Queen Elizabeth) on 29 October 1929. It was damaged during the war and removed. Happily a replacement seat was installed on 21 November 1979 in the presence of the Duke of Devonshire. It lies just across the road from the *Beachy Head Hotel*, and looks less out of place than the original.

Byfield on piano, cello Louis Cramer, organ Frederick Cramer and bass Tom Hinkinson. The gala broadcasts were economical for the BBC: a microphone was suspended from that delicate chandelier and the sound was perfect.'[19]

Mrs Clara Johns was not only a national bowls champion, for thanks to her women's bowling became firmly established on a national scale. Cyril James Hastings Tolley, the British Amateur Golf Champion in 1920 and 1929, lived locally as a child, and later served as an Eastbourne councillor from 1958 to 1962.

In 1929 Caffyn's sold 1,000 cars in a year for the first time. A Caffyn's publicity booklet stated firmly, 'Caffyn's will only act as agents for British cars – they are not prepared to stock or push the sale of foreign cars'. This exclusive involvement with British marques lasted until 1977 when the company acquired Fiat and Mercedes Benz franchises. In 1930 the National Provincial bank bought the *Royal Hotel* (formerly *Railway Hotel* and Kinburn House) to build their new Eastbourne branch. The new bank was given decorative ceilings by C.G. Garrard. The Star Brewery used the £30,000 it received from the sale to build both the *Prince Albert* in Old Town and the *Horse and Groom* at Polegate, two rewarding ventures.

Many residents cruised every winter, keeping on a butler, housekeeper, cook, maids and gardeners. Poverty existed in the town, but not on the scale of elsewhere, and, after a collection was made for the unemployed, clothing and £1,000 was sent to South Wales. The families of local unemployed were also assisted, £1,530 being distributed to over 120 persons.

102 In 1925 the Corporation deemed that telephone kiosks on the seafront should have thatched roofs to match the rustic public shelters. This one was by the Redoubt. After 1936 they were replaced by standard phone boxes. (Photograph G. Clark)

103 Typical shop display in Station Parade *c.*1925. Before refrigerators, shops could not keep their perishables over the weekend. On a Saturday night at Gales, the fishmongers, a man would stand up on a box and declare, 'I tell yer what I'll do, I'll slap a pair of kippers in with this for a shilling the lot, how about that?' This is what the crowds had waited to hear.

Amy Johnson, the popular female aviator, landed at Kings Drive 'aerodrome' in 1930, and the Prince of Wales, later Duke of Windsor, flew in, on 30 June 1931, to Frowd's Field (now the Park College site), which was also used by Sir Alan Cobham's Flying Circus. The Prince came to unveil a tablet commemorating the purchase (at last) of the Devonshire Park Floral Hall, Indian Pavilion, house and skating rink, for £30,000, lay a foundation stone for an extension to the Princess Alice Hospital and open Prince's Park.

The stars of the theatre also came to Eastbourne. Muriel Childs saw Fay Compton at the Devonshire Park Theatre, and Ivor Novello and Cicely Courtneidge were at the Pier Theatre: at the Royal Hippodrome, first house 4½d. for children, 'I saw Harry Tate and his famous motoring sketch, G.H. Elliot, "The Chocolate-coloured Coon", and Wilson, Kepple and Betty doing their sand dance. With no over-exposure from TV, some of the turns toured the country doing the same act for years.' Murray King was at the Devonshire Park Theatre from 1894 to 1935, where his pantomine Transformation Scenes were 'brilliantly contrived'. Beale's, Dale & Kerley, Bobby's and Plummer Roddis all vied to provide the most fantastic Christmas Grotto, and Beale's organised the arrival of their Father Christmas at the station. Crowds watched as he was driven to the store, with a suitably heavy sack, in a decorated carriage drawn by white horses.

At the end of 1931 Messrs Pirelli made a claim against Eastbourne Corporation in respect of electrical contracts, but bribery was suspected.[20] In April 1933 Pirelli Ltd., Richard Chatfield, ex-Alderman, David Roberts, ex-Deputy Borough Electrical Engineer, and Mr Reed, an official of Pirelli's, pleaded guilty to various charges, and Mr Chatfield and Mr Roberts were each fined £250, Mr Reed £50 and Pirelli £550. The Salvation Army opened the Citadel, Central Avenue in July 1932 and built a hall in Royal Sussex Crescent in 1935.

Edward Marjoribanks was Conservative Unionist MP from 1929 until he shot himself in 1932, and his successor, Conservative MP John Slater, died of a heart attack at a public banquet on 15 February 1935. Charles Taylor (later knighted) was elected unopposed and lasted until 1974, overstaying his welcome as far as some were concerned.

104   Will, Tom and Fred Allchorn spratting. Before 1939 fishing was an occupation of most boatmen in the winter. The boat on the right is *Lest We Forget*, named after George Allchorn who was killed at the Dardanelles in 1915. The early 1930s were difficult times: Speedboats, one of the Eastbourne boat companies, went bankrupt along with H.A. Dossor, the jeweller, J.H. Gooden, milliner, and Gilbert Soddy, baker, an ex-mayor of Eastbourne.

The year Hitler became Chancellor of Germany was the Golden Jubilee of the Incorporation of the Borough of Eastbourne. Lachlan Maclachlan, the mayor in 1933, unfortunately had a heart attack at a Council meeting just beforehand and missed all the excitement. His family ran the Scotch Bakery into the 1960s and, as was the custom, lived over the original shop. The Jubilee was commemorated by a week of events in June which included church services, a school pageant and a tea for the town's infants (the commemorative mug was presented later

because of the atrocious weather), and 250 old people went to the Picturedrome. They had a high tea afterwards and were presented with half a pound of tea (women) or a packet of tobacco (men). There was also a carnival procession, an Air Rally and parades.[21]

Mrs Helen Hornby Lewis, a 'quiet millionairess' who lived in South Cliff, left land 'for the perpetual use and enjoyment of the public', and the Corporation laid out Helen Garden with a bowling green and 18-hole putting course. This completed

105 'About 1931 I saw the *Graf Zeppelin* pass along the coast. The silvery cigar was enormous, it seemed to fill the sky. People said they knew why it came – to take photographs of our naval installations, and they were probably right.' (Photograph G. Clark)

the Lawns and prevented any development of the area, which would have been 'a great detriment to Eastbourne's amenities'. In 1935 Lord Leconfield officially opened the gardens and the new band-stand on the same day.

Sir James Purves Stewart, an internationally acclaimed neurologist who had lived in Eastbourne from 1882 to 1899, bought the Belle Tout lighthouse in 1923 for £1,500. He refurbished it, and entertained King George V and Queen Mary to the views in March 1935. Their Silver Jubilee in May 1935 was celebrated in a similar style to the Incorporation Jubilee church service, day off for Corporation employees (with pay), children and old folk taken to the cinema, fireworks, morris dancing, floodlighting and a Beachy Head beacon, all for £851.

A round booking hall was added to Eastbourne station, shops were inserted into the Terminus Road

façade, and on 7 July 1935 Caroline Allchorn (née Breach), who lived to be 100, welcomed the first electric train into the station. It was driven by Cllr J. Wheeler, who became mayor of Eastbourne, unknown for a railwayman. Eastbourne's mayors were usually described as 'gentleman', or 'farmer', or 'retired from the Indian Civil Service'. As Paul Harris put it, 'The town appeared to be under the control of people who knew each other because their professions crossed paths, or who met in Masonic, political, or club circles.'

Schools and churches still flourished. Peter Palmer says, 'Before the war Eastbourne had about thirty private schools and school crocodiles were often seen.' Eric 'Gilbert & Sullivan' Laming, head of Neville House, insisted that his pupils processed in Indian file, no doubt because of the narrow pavements, although there were those who implied that his extended crocodile was to promote the

106 Pioneer aviatrix Amy Johnson landing her plane, the all-green *Jason*, at Frowds Field along Kings Drive in 1930. She set many air records, but was probably shot down by 'Friendly Fire' over the Thames in 1941 when ferrying aircraft for war service. Her husband, Jim Mollison, force landed at Pevensey in August 1931 on his way from Australia to Croydon in 8 days 22 hours.

107 Programme for the Prince of Wales' visit in 1931. A desolate 28 acres of Crumbles shingle and ponds, originally leased from the Davies Gilberts, was made into a shallow boating lake and an 18-hole miniature golf course, while the Oval football pitch and athletic track were built nearby. It was called the Gilbert Recreation Ground until the Prince of Wales planted a tree and renamed it Prince's Park.

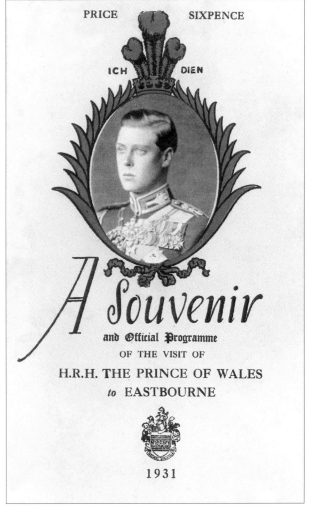

PRICE   SIXPENCE

ICH   DIEN

A Souvenir

and Official Programme

OF THE VISIT OF

H.R.H. THE PRINCE OF WALES

to EASTBOURNE

1931

impression of a thriving school. Eliza Watson left £80,000 for a new church, and St Elisabeth's Church, Victoria Drive was finally consecrated by Bishop George Bell on 19 February 1938, although it has always had structural problems.

Caleb Diplock 'junior' finally died in 1936 at the age of 95, unmarried and without issue, leaving £527,936. He had minimal involvement with his father's Eastbourne brewery. He believed that he had no dependants and his solicitor drew up a will leaving his money to 'benevolent and charitable' institutions, and most went to hospitals selected by his executors. In 1940 the will was challenged and eventually the House of Lords determined that the charities had to return monies received, while 48 distant relatives benefited. The unravelling took until 1950.

108   The PS *Brighton Queen,* one of P.&A. Campbell's boats that called regularly at the pier. 'For half-a-guinea we went to Boulogne on the *Devonia,* one of Campbell's paddle boats. There was a little band playing on deck and an observation platform to view the pistons driving the paddle-wheels.'

109   The new bandstand, built at a cost of £29,000 to replace 'The Birdcage'. It was designed to seat 3,000, but the story goes that on 5 August 1935, when it was officially opened by Lord Leconfield, Lord Lieutenant of the County, 10,400 people paid for chairs.

110   The 'Round the Bay' boat, *Enchantress*, in 1937/8. She was lost at Dunkirk. Back row: Jack Allchorn, Bill Kent, Fred Allchorn, Tom Allchorn, the Hon. Gerald Lascelles (passenger), Sam Allchorn and 'Hollands' Huggett. In front: John Hill, Fred and Nelson Hurd, Alec Huggett, Bill Boniface and William Allchorn. Before 1939 Allchorn's ran up to five boats, each carrying thirty to forty passengers, notable among whom in 1937 was Haile Selasse, the Emperor of Ethiopia.

Life remained tough on the local farms.[22] Prices were lower than 100 years before, so the 1920s and '30s were hand-to-mouth years when produce had to be sold before the weekly groceries could be bought. Yet the economic situation was improving, and the visit in 1936 of the Duke and Duchess of York, with the little princesses, brought a little extra brightness. The Terriss Memorial

Lifeboathouse opened on 22 March 1937, the first lifeboat museum in the UK, with Lady Seymour Hicks, daughter of Terriss, in attendance. It now contains memorabilia of the bombed SS *Barnhill*, and the Eastbourne lifeboat which was to sail to Dunkirk.

The Royal Ladies' Golf Club closed that year, but the main event was the coronation of King

111 Eastbourne Girls' High School at Gildredge Park, during the town's coronation celebrations. Old people and the blind, deaf and dumb were given a dinner at the Town Hall, and 2,300 junior schoolchildren were given tea, and entertained by Clarkson Rose. The senior children elected to buy 'wireless sets' for the school, or present the money to a school in a distressed area. The mayor presented 3,980 mugs and 1,242 penknives to the children. Aquatic displays, popular at the time, were held at Prince's Park, and Ran Dan races and sculling competitions were held for fishermen and boatmen.

George VI and Queen Elizabeth on 10 May 1937. Schoolchildren gave performances of Coronation Cavalcade, and there were dances at the Town Hall and a ball at the Winter Garden; territorial units fired a *feu de joie* at Gildredge Park; the Town Hall had a Grand Historical Procession, and there was a fireworks display when local boats (and much else) were lit up.[23] On Empire Day, two weeks later, over 4,000 schoolchildren marched past the mayor in Gildredge Park. Douglas Swift says of Empire Day celebrated on Queen Victoria's birthday from her reign up to 1946, 'At school we paraded waving our Union flags and singing patriotic songs, we had a half-day holiday and thought it grand. We liked looking at the world map with all the red bits saying, "That's ours, and that", and we were proud of our position in the world.'

The local fishing industry was ending.[24] The Hide family connection finished in the 1930s, and by 2000 not one of the town's old families was in fishing. In 1937 the Bill for the extension of Eastbourne received Royal Assent, bringing part of Willingdon and much of Langney into the town. The Superannuation Act of that year essentially allowed loyal servants such as Town Clerk H.W. Fovargue to retire, after 48 years, 'at 3d. in the £1 on the rates'. In other ways Eastbourne had changed little. Bathchairs plied for hire on the front, 'The Major' rode his piebald horse up and down from the *Grand Hotel* to the pier, and the tarred surface of Victoria Drive stopped at Downs Avenue. There was a family atmosphere in the town: Ron Spicer says, 'I would avoid going along Terminus Road; you could hardly move without meeting people and having to

112 Eastbourne's stalwart Police Force in 1938, with Chief Constable W.H. Smith. Despite 'the antics of Mr. Hitler', building went ahead locally as economic conditions improved, and in February 1938 the main police station in Grove Road was completed at a total cost of £49,433.

talk.' Betty Palmer adds, 'Bobby's store had a broad elegant staircase to the restaurant where there was a three-piece orchestra. The tea rooms were places for socialising, on a Saturday morning you would meet a dozen people you knew.'

Eastbourne was providing a good range of entertainment for visitors too. While business had been affected by the slump, Eastbourne's bands, deckchairs and sea bathing produced a surplus of over £8,000, easily covering a small loss on the Devonshire Baths, and the buses too made a profit. An indoor bowling green was one need which was not satisfied until 1978 despite requests. Standards were maintained and a planning application for the site of Ascham St Vincent's School, in Meads, was turned down because the proposed housing density would exceed two houses per acre.[25] The Council was firmly Tory and the membership seldom changed, which gave a

continuity and reduced the need to go vote chasing; they introduced a free school milk service in 1939 which was finely tailored for 'necessitous children'. They also renamed Seaside Road, between Memorial Square and Terminus Road, transforming it into Trinity Trees.

Before 1939 the New Year was greeted by a cacophony of sound. Steam locomotives blew their whistles, and the gas works blew their hooters. When few people had watches they were also used to call staff to work and to indicate meal times. Now they have gone, along with the Snoot Parade and much else, although the Duke of Devonshire continues to keep an eye on the town.

The Munich euphoria was fading. People wished devoutly for anything that would prevent another war, but the dramatic display of the Northern Lights which occurred in January 1939 was regarded as the harbinger of disaster.

Five

The Most Bombed Town on the South Coast

The town was well ahead with its Second World War preparations; over 60,000 gas masks had been distributed, and the first air-raid siren trials (albeit steam-driven) had been held on 28 July 1938, but Eastbourne expected war to be much the same as 1914-18. Hadn't the MP, Charles Taylor, expressed it clearly enough in the spring of 1939? 'Attackers would not go to the trouble of carrying high-explosive bombs for Eastbourne.' Air Raid Precautions, or ARP, were taken seriously, bearing in mind that Londoners expected raids with poison gas as soon as war was declared, but Eastbourne was designated a Safety Zone and warned to receive evacuees from London if war came.

The horrors of war, however, came early to the town. On August Bank Holiday, 1939, in an augury of the messy times ahead, an RAF Blenheim bomber on exercises from Wattisham, Suffolk crashed into Beachy Head cliff in heavy mist. The crew of three, and a young woman who just happened to be walking on the cliffs, were killed. Trainloads of evacuees started arriving at Eastbourne on Friday 1 September, and poured in over three days. Little Londoners, with their name-labels, pregnant mums and the infirm were all moved on by bus, car and ambulance to billets in private homes or hospitals. For the children the excitement of a free trip to the seaside was wearing off by now, replaced by bewilderment and tearfulness, especially as every child underwent a medical examination, and head lice were common.

Some businesses evacuated themselves to this safe haven. The National Amalgamated Approved Society's staff came from London to the empty Temple Grove School buildings. Including those who made their own way, almost 20,000 descended on the town, adding about a third to its population.

The local authority under the Town Clerk, Frank Busby, one of those wonderful municipal officials who ran the place, had everything under control.

Eastbourne's war, like everybody else's, started with the 'phoney war' from September 1939 to the early summer of 1940. The blackout was unpopular and road traffic accidents soared, but 'Put that Light Out' became the catchphrase and, as early as 20 September, a Willingdon resident was fined £10 for showing a light.

Apart from an unpatriotic epidemic of German measles in the cold 1939-40 winter, Eastbourne's first taste of action and bravery came in March 1940 off Beachy Head. German planes put a bomb down the funnel of the 5,430 ton SS *Barnhill* carrying a mixed cargo of cheeses, tinned stews and beans. It drifted out of control and ran aground near Langney Point. The lifeboat took off the survivors, but later in the day the uncanny sound of the ship's bell was heard from the shore so it set out again with Dr Duncan Churcher aboard. Two lifeboatmen scrambled onto the red-hot plates of the stricken ship and found that the captain, blown off the bridge and assumed missing, had managed to crawl back and grip the ship's bell rope with his teeth, in spite of extensive injuries. Another lifeboatman described the scene in the shallow water: 'One moment the *Barnhill* would be towering above us, showering sparks and molten metal, and the next we would be riding on the wave and almost level with the deck.' Captain Michael O'Neill was taken to hospital and lived to return to thank the town. His rescuers, Alec Huggett and Tom Allchorn, were awarded RNLI Bronze Medals.

Even so, it seemed that for Eastbourne the war would be much the same as the earlier conflict. At the AGM of the *Grand Hotel* in 1940 the chairman,

113 The SS *Barnhill* was hit by German bombs on 20 March 1940, killing four of the crew and setting the ship on fire. While Fire Brigade tenders tackled the flames, Eastbourne's lifeboat coxswain, Mike Hardy, took off 28 of the crew, eight of whom had to be admitted to hospital, where one died; he is buried in Langney cemetery. The remnants of the *Barnhill* have almost disappeared, but tales of the cargo washed ashore are persistent. The locals, on rations, were delighted to 'liberate' the goods, and as the labels had soaked off the tins the contents were a surprise.

Cecil Page, told shareholders that up to May 1940 business had been excellent. Eastbourne's small craft helped in the May-June 1940 evacuation from France, and two pleasure boats and a fishing boat were lost. The *Jane Holland* lifeboat truly demonstrated the Bulldog spirit in the course of her Dunkirk experience. She was hit by over 500 missiles, was rammed, and finally abandoned. Two days later she was found floating in the Channel by the Royal Navy and towed to Dover where she was repaired and returned to Eastbourne to serve for another nine years.[1]

Overnight Eastbourne went from Safety Zone to Front Line. People were prohibited from enter-ing a coastal belt and were turned back if they were not residents or did not have business there. Mothers-to-be, when due, were packed up country to East Grinstead, but Mrs Olive Pack's baby was born prematurely, and when her husband, in the Queen's Royal Regiment, tried to visit her in St Mary's Hospital he was not allowed past Polegate crossroads.

The foreshore was dotted with poles, spikes and wire to stop planes landing, and the beach was mined. Nigel Quiney recalls, 'I didn't learn to swim until after the war because children weren't allowed near the beaches.' All non-combatants were told to keep a case packed so they could leave immediately

114 Dunkirk survivors at St Mary's Hospital. Hundreds of Dunkirk casualties were succoured in Eastbourne. Nurse Madge Hogan, on night duty and smarting from sun-bathing on the Downs earlier in the day, was confronted by stacks of blood-stained stretchers, helmets, packs and rifles. 'The sight of C ward packed tight with soldiers will remain with me forever. They were boys of 18, 19 and 20, and I was only 20. One lad with a bullet in his brain thought I was an angel when I gave him a drink. He died the next day. I still reproach myself with the thought that I should have been more concerned about the welfare of his soul.'

if they heard the ringing of the church bells, the invasion signal. The Army came to blow up the pier while Clarkson Rose's end-of-the-pier show *Twinkle* was running. They were persuaded to wait until the end of the performance, by which time they agreed not to destroy it but to confuse the Germans completely by removing planking and installing a machine-gun over the theatre and a Bofors gun at the pier entrance.

On 21 July 1940 over 3,000 Eastbourne children were sent to the Home Counties. Eastbourne had no defences and no shelters, apart from a few Anderson shelters[2] and strengthened cellars under the larger stores for customers caught in a raid.[3] Two First World War six-inch naval guns were mounted at the base of the Wish Tower. The remaining 24 students at Ranny's School of Domestic Economy went to Caterham and the Royal Navy took over, but Ranny said if you take over the school you take me over too and throughout the war she and a small staff cooked for the sailors of 'HMS Ranny'. It is said no unit was luckier in their billet.

The first phase of bombing, from 3 July 1940 to 7 June 1941, opened for real on the morning of Sunday 7 July, when a single, low-flying Dornier Do17 dropped high-explosive bombs along Whitley Road from St Philip's Avenue to Avondale Road.

Over the subsequent months, as the Battle of Britain raged overhead, Eastbourne copped a raid almost every day. On 16 August 1940 the latticework of vapour trails, the roar of engines, the rattle of machine-guns above, and the crump of bombs below, were complemented by a Messerschmitt Me110 screaming out of the sky to dive into the grounds of the Aldro School at Meads. This raid stimulated the town to hit back, and the *Eastbourne Gazette and Herald* sponsored a Spitfire Fund. A Spitfire cost £5,000, the price of ten houses of the day, and within a week Eastbourne had raised £6,000.

These early attacks generated indignation for it was felt that Eastbourne was not a legitimate target. This soon changed as troops were stationed in the town, the Downs were used for training, radar equipment blossomed on Beachy Head, fighting vehicles were tested for amphibious use, and the area was used as a staging post for raids into France. A proclamation of 10 September stated that anyone without duty could leave and many went, including a few who did have duties. The population fell from 60,000 to around 10,000, and grass grew in the centre of town roads.

The railway station was crowded on Friday 13 September with people being evacuated when the town was raided by at least five planes.

115 Weekend exercise for D Company, Eastbourne Home Guard, at Park Avenue, 1942. In 1940 Anthony Eden had called upon ex-soldiers and those over 16 to form a new force, the Local Defence Volunteers or LDV. It was christened 'Look, Duck, and Vanish', so the new Prime Minister, Winston Churchill, renamed it the Home Guard. Ex-soldiers abounded in Eastbourne, all in fear of Wehrmacht parachutists desecrating the town, so 2,000 volunteered.

116 Mr W.H. Kefford describes Eastbourne's first bomb: 'On Sunday morning, about 11 o'clock, my brother-in-law and I were walking by St Philip's Church, when a plane, at no great height, came over. Reg yelled, "It's a German, get down," and pulled me behind a wall. We were about 30 metres from one of the bombs.' Ronald Turner records, 'We heard the sound of a plane and as I went to the door there came a terrifying screaming sound, a loud explosion and the house fell on us. I struggled out of the rubble to find myself in the garden, looking at the mantelpiece from the front bedroom, and saw that our house was non-existent. I was in hospital for three weeks, my mother for five and my father died there.'

117 An Me110 shot down on 16 August 1940 crashed into Meads. Ernst Hollekamp, the pilot, jumped too late and landed on the roof of Hillbrow School. The body is being lowered down by the Fire Brigade. His widow visited the spot after the war. The observer/gunner, Richard Schurk, fell into the sea off Holywell and was left to drown. Other casualties were three men collecting scrap metal who had taken shelter under their van; all were killed.

118 'At about five o'clock on 31 August there was a loud bang in Wish Road with not a plane in sight.' Army Intelligence found fragments of a 4-inch shell, and after the war it was confirmed from German sources that a U-boat on a photographic reconnaissance for the invasion had fired to obscure the reason behind its visit. It also shelled Cuckmere Haven, along the coast, the proposed landing spot for the 6th Mountain Division in the German invasion plan 'Operation Sea Lion'.

119 Christ Church School burnt out after being hit by an oil bomb on 13 September 1940, 'Black Friday, the start of the real trouble'.

Bombs dropped on Seaside and the town centre, and in Hyde Road and Gildredge Road solicitor's offices were destroyed and legal papers were found in Pevensey Road, half a mile away. Two 250kg. bombs fell on Seaside recreation ground, one failing to explode. The next day two Spitfires attacked a Dornier bomber over the town and sent it into the sea, but otherwise it was a day of noise, dust and debris. At 1320, 1400, 1430 and 1515 hours German aircraft dropped HE and incendiary bombs over the town, from the *Burlington Hotel* on the front to Old Town, and from Lottbridge Drove on the east to Meads in the west, and later three Dorniers attacked the Beachy Head radar.

Saturday 28 September witnessed scenes of exceptional gallantry and courage. Four bombs hit Tideswell Road, Bourne Street and Cavendish Place, where eight people were trapped in cellars. Surgeon Laurence Snowball said, 'Five were rescued, but a 17-year-old Hankham girl – I still recall her name, Miss Peggy Harland – was pinned by a steel girder across her ankles.' She was in great pain, and unable to move, yet she kept up her spirits and those of her toiling rescuers. 'After 24 hours, when it was apparent that she could not be released, Dr Roy Barron and myself crawled to her, he to give the anaesthetic and me to amputate both her legs. Sadly, Miss Harland died in hospital two days later.' She was posthumously awarded the Girl Guides

120 A Latimer Road house after 15 September 1940. The rear wall has been blown away but the bed remains balanced precariously and, incredibly, the dressing table has a bowl and ewer in place and apparently untouched.

121 Cavendish Place, 28 September 1940. The rescue squads strove to reach trapped victims but their work was hampered by a burst water main only kept in check by continuous pumping. They knew, too, that an unexploded bomb lay close by.

122 At about 4p.m., on 8 October 1940, Pauline Markquick was waiting with her mother at the Southdown depôt in Susans Road for a bus home, when Harold Bobby's department store was bombed. 'The siren had gone, so we stood back from the roadway, but we weren't going to miss our place in the queue. There was an incredible noise. Although probably not the safest thing to do, we rushed out of the depôt, as you do. You couldn't see along Lismore Road for a cloud of dust and particles.'

Gilt Cross, and 14 gallantry awards were made to the rescuers.[4]

Harry Homewood of the rescue services described his experience when Pickford's in Commercial Road was bombed, and a solid raft of concrete had to be jacked up before a man could be released. 'I crawled in and found his legs had been squashed, but my main hindrance was the tin-tacks scattered from the upholstery store. I splinted his legs, but when I tried to ease my way out with him I found my route blocked by another rescuer. He was so petrified with fear that the jacks would collapse on him that he was unable to move.

We finally conveyed the injured man to hospital where he recovered.'

Raids continued most days, with dead and injured in almost every raid, and some close shaves too. On 10 October a high-flying Junkers Ju88 scored a direct hit on St Mary's Church, Decoy Drive. It demolished the building, apart from the bell tower, but there were no casualties, although only a short time before the church had been filled with people using it as a communal dining centre. There were also the unfortunate incidents: one woman died of coal gas poisoning when nearby bombs fractured a gas main that ran underneath her

123 On 8 October a 250kg. bomb fell in North Street (top left), just behind Dale & Kerley's store (now T.J. Hughes), but the fuse (the whitish round spot on the bomb) was jammed and could not be removed (top right), so the unexploded bomb was dug out and removed live (above and middle right). Wilf Bignell photographed every phase of the digging out and removal of the bomb. The final picture (right) shows how the fuse should be removed – with care. Some bombs did not explode because they had not been primed; others were delayed action – timed to go off about three hours after being dropped; others had various booby trap devices to blow up anyone brave enough to attempt to render them inactive. The sergeant of this squad was killed by a UXB on 26 October.

house.[5] There was so much damage around Bourne Street that it was known as 'Bomb Alley', or 'Hell Fire Corner'. Venn Claydon said, 'If you were brave enough to walk along Terminus Road, it was not exceptional to go all the way from the station to Bolton Road without seeing a single passer-by.'

Many buildings were commandeered. What is now Upperton United Reformed Church housed bombed-out families; All Saints' Hospital was used for troops once again; and the Acacia Villa clinic in Wartling Road became a Civil Defence First Aid Station. Mr B.H. Wright of Langney Farm found that his guard post was the old Smallpox Hospital, just east of the new Sovereign harbour. Not used since an outbreak in 1929, it was demolished in 1946. Empty schools and hotels were taken over by the Army, RAF and Navy. The *Rustington Court Hotel* was a WRNS billet, the *Lansdowne* the Home Guard HQ, Eastbourne College and Granville House School housed the Royal Navy, and Roborough School in Upper Avenue had Canadians. The WAAF occupied the *Mostyn* hotel until it

124 The test card of the German TV from Paris picked up by monitors at Beachy Head. The headland was used to extend the range of the radio telephone communications with Allied planes, especially those pin-pointing the position of airmen downed in the Channel, for whom high-speed rescue launches set out from Newhaven. Direction-finding equipment had been set up on Warren Hill in March 1941, and, later, Chain Home Low radar stations on the cliff attempted to detect low-flying planes.

was bombed in March 1943; the site is now *Grand Court*.

Despite much damage the casualties were few compared with the loss of life in the Coventry raid, due almost certainly to the evacuation of the town. The locals had not lost their sense of humour: after one incident a man called at the *Cavendish* saloon bar for stiff refreshment but, as he put it, 'On reaching the door I saw that an unexploded bomb [UXB] had beaten me to it, but had not yet attracted the barman's attention'.[6] By now petrol rationing was severe and most people left their cars in the garage, jacked up on bricks 'for the duration'. A regulation, strictly applied in coastal towns, was that on leaving the car for any length of time it had to be immobilised by removing the rotor arm of the distributor.

Laurence Snowball said, 'I attended quite a number of airmen with burns who had crash landed on the emergency airfield at Friston, and a few German airmen with broken legs who had bailed out at insufficient height.[7] Most were very reasonable, but I recall one truculent pilot who insisted on being transferred to a German hospital in the area of Britain that had been captured. We managed to convince him otherwise with the help of our junior Medical Officer who, strange as it may seem, was German. Dr Katz, an anti-Nazi, had escaped from Germany only a few days before the war and, after a spell in an internment camp, he worked hard as our only junior doctor. I believe he went on to be a leading paediatrician in the United States, but his fluent German was a greater asset than his medical knowledge on that occasion.'

There had not been an invasion – yet – but Eastbourne's raids continued, the majority from bombers abandoning a raid on London. In April 1941 the future Duke and Duchess of Devonshire spent their two-week honeymoon in Eastbourne. Lord Andrew Cavendish, as he was, on leave from the Coldstream Guards, recalled, 'We heard the bombers flying overhead at night. It was an eerie sound which we will never forget.'

John Claremont writes, 'In February 1942 I arrived in the town as an RAF aircrew cadet for a course on navigation. We took sights with a sextant and retired to our rooms in the *Cavendish Hotel* to work out our position; the first time I did the calculation Eastbourne had moved to Hertfordshire.' On 4 May the east wing of the *Cavendish* was hit when Eastbourne's next phase of air raids, the terrifying 'Hit-and-Run' or 'Tip-and-Run' attacks started. Nine bomb-carrying Me109 fighters flew low over the Channel, lifted over Beachy Head and swept across the town. The bombs struck the railway line, the station, St John's Church and a gas holder. On the run home the planes fired at a fishing boat in the bay, badly wounding fishermen Alec Huggett and Micky Andrews. What incensed the locals was William Joyce, Lord Haw-Haw, broadcasting that night on 'Jarmany Calling', describing their boat as an armed trawler. But rumours were an essential part of wartime life, from 'The Germans have landed' to 'There are oranges at the greengrocers'. It wasn't fantasy, however, to say that the radar units on Beachy Head could view German TV.[8]

On 13 May 1942 King George VI visited his Armoured Division on the Eastbourne Downs, although the town only learnt of it later. The bodies of unknown seamen killed in the channel and washed ashore were buried in churchyards around the coast. We know HM trawler *Aventurine* sank one mile off Beachy Head on 1 December 1943, and U413 was destroyed there towards the end of the war. News was received of the loss at sea of Eric Ravilious, an Eastbourne artist famed for his distinctive pictures of submarines. With the Battle of the Atlantic not going well, everyone was encouraged to grow more food – Dig for Victory. Every plot became a vegetable patch: Gildredge Park was dug over and the Carpet Gardens grew onions. The Downs were ploughed almost up to the cliff edge in the drive to produce more food, but even hay-making had its risks; Derrick Pyle recalls diving for cover: 'There was low cloud, the threshing machine was whirling away, and the first we noticed was when we saw spurts of earth across the field as the planes fired their cannon shells.' Locals thought the German pilots switched off their engines as they came in, and started them again to make their escape, but they were not able to restart their engines in the air.[9]

Derek Keay recalls walking by Motcombe baths in Old Town when a Focke-Wulf FW190 swept over with guns firing. 'My wife and I dived in

125 A bus raked by machine-gun fire from low-flying aircraft. Not surprisingly, the driver was killed. The remaining headlight shows the standard blackout masking. Car lights consisted of low power rear and side lights, masked to one inch diameter and hooded with baffled slots so that not a glimmer could be seen at a height of two inches above the light. You were not allowed to use a torch during a raid, and there were stories of people parking their cars and not being able to find them until the next day.

somewhere, but we could hear the bullets hitting the roof of the shelter. Another time we were near the main Post Office in Upperton Road when six Me109s strafed Terminus Road and Upperton. It was most frightening.'

Arthur Edward Rush, Eastbourne's mayor at the outbreak of war, was an independent councillor re-elected in November 1939 and again from 1940 to 1942. He worked in a quiet, unassuming manner, consoling bombed-out victims and getting things done, and was a leader in the campaign for a local air-raid warning for the town. There had been no warning of the first raid on Eastbourne, in July 1940, and by the autumn air-raid warnings were a joke; as one victim put it, 'Just as I arrived at the hospital the air-raid siren sounded the alarm.' Stanley Apps remembers waiting for a bus in Eldon Road: 'There was no siren, and suddenly three

126 Mrs Elizabeth Bugler strides past the Marks & Spencer's site in Terminus Road flattened in a lunchtime attack on Friday 18 December 1942. Nine of the rescuers were injured trying to recover the victims. Derek Keay said, 'The Marks and Sparks bomb was very sad in that over 50 women and children were killed or hurt and so near Christmas. It spoilt the holiday for everybody. Afterwards, as you walked past, troops were clearing up the rubble and when they found a till you would see them empty it into their pockets.'

planes came round the Beehive Plantation and started firing at Old Town.'

In a way it was understandable. After an erroneous alert at the beginning of the war caused by a single French aircraft, sirens were not sounded for single aircraft, which didn't help Eastbourne. The air-raid warning area controller was 30 miles away and hence Eastbourne endured unheralded bombing. It was too easy for German planes to sweep in low and dash away before any authorised alarm. At last, representations by the Town Council and the local press led to a local siren that gave about half-a-minute's warning, enough to dash for cover. This separate 'Cuckoo' warning, so-called after the noise it made, was first heard on 6 June 1942.

An attack on 11 August 1942 was Eastbourne's heaviest night raid. Flares from waves of bombers lit up the town and HE and incendiary bombs caused widespread damage. Seaside, Meads, Babylon Down, Grove Road, The Avenue, the railway station, Terminus Road and Willingdon were hard hit, and St Anne's Church burnt out. It was a week before Operation Jubilee, the ill-fated Dieppe raid of 19 August, and many thought the Germans had got wind of the attack. The Canadians were practising tank battles and artillery firing on the Downs, and Newhaven was a departure port for the raid.[10] Chaseley, in South Cliff, was also the 1st

Canadian Special Wireless Section's control centre for communications during the raid, and part of the fighter cover took off from Friston airfield, two of these planes being lost, so Eastbourne was a fair enough target.[11]

FW190 fighter-bombers struck again and again. On 13 August they crossed the coast at Cooden and came in from the east, and on 16 September they had another go at the station, killing six railwaymen. These raids confirmed that the fighter-bombers, such as Me109s, carrying medium-capacity 250kg. bombs, were more accurate than high-level bombers, and that the FW190, which could carry a 1,000kg. bomb load, had become such a menace that a Spitfire squadron was later installed at Friston airfield.

It was not uncommon for hospitals to treat 50 casualties at a time, working with windows blown in. If numerous casualties occurred over a day or two those who had been patched up were sent by ambulance to inland hospitals. Stanley Apps' opinion was that, 'In the Hit-and-Run raids you didn't have time to go into a shelter, you just dived under a table. It wasn't a normal life, but it became normal.' A few indoor Morrison shelters were issued, but not enough, so the Borough Surveyor enterprisingly produced a wooden-framed replica. This was ridiculed until both types were tested by dropping a load of bricks on them and the local shelter stood up to the weight better than the metal-framed Morrison.

Mrs Ruth Tucker has memories of the bombing of 4 June 1943, when the Technical Institute and shops were hit. 'I went out to find that scattered all along The Avenue were books from the library and fish from MacFisheries. People were picking up food for both mind and body.' Don't think that people didn't enjoy themselves. Gordon Rider's band played almost nightly at the Winter Gardens and with so many troops training on the Downs there was no shortage of partners for local women. Golfers were able to fit in a round too, although upright poles driven into the fairways to catch invading gliders could also deflect the occasional golf ball.

One popular recreation that assisted the war effort was helping with the harvest. Farmer Lewis Pyle of

127 Nurses on the roof of St Mary's Hospital in 1942 wearing their tin hats. A workman on the roof had been machine-gunned by low-flying planes. The nurses with badges were Civil Nursing Reserve, 23 of whom helped on the wards; although most had little training, they were welcome and formed about a third of the nursing staff.

128 The raid of 15 January 1943, when four FW190s dived over the town from Beachy Head firing their cannon. They dropped a 500kg. bomb each and effectively obliterated Cross Street and Duke Street. This tactic was repeated on 23 January (when one enemy plane was shot down over Cow Gap) and again on 7 February, when five NFS firemen and a firewoman were killed. Five are buried together at Langney.

129   Grove Road, looking towards Ivy Terrace, 4 June 1943. You can almost smell the dust in the immediacy of the bombing. The worst raid for civilian casualties was in April, when over 30 were killed and nearly 100 injured. Greatest loss of life occurred when a surface shelter was hit. Venn Claydon wrote, 'The main nuisances were the Tip-and-Run raiders whom we took to be pilots wearing the flying equivalent of L-plates. They came over at a low altitude to avoid detection by radar, dropped their bombs, gave a burst of their guns, and returned unscathed.'

Chalk Farm welcomed family parties. 'As we played our small part to bring the harvest safely home, high overhead, scarcely audible, our bombers were setting out. We did not have to be reminded that many would not be coming back.' In February 1944 the damaged US Liberator bomber *Ruthless* was almost home when it crashed into Butt's Brow near Willingdon.

It is possible that Eastbourne received the first casualties from the Normandy landings. Early on 6 June 1944 an aircraft carrying paratroopers over France was peppered when an anti-aircraft shell burst underneath. Ordered to return, it just managed to bellyflop at Friston airfield. Mr Snowball noted that, 'At the hospital we spent the rest of the night digging out bits of shrapnel, and all they did was

to bemoan their disappointment at missing the invasion.'[12]

The first of Hitler's Victory weapons, or V1s, came next. The first flying bomb, or PAC (Pilotless Aircraft), was seen from Beachy Head on the night of 12/13 June heading for London, where most of them were targeted. Eastbourne and the south coast received misdirected and malfunctioning ones, and a mere 15 landed in the Borough; although much damage was caused to property and many civilians were injured, none died.

Over the next two months there was an incident every few days, and Eastbourne residents learnt to listen out for the sound of the engine. If it kept going the 'Doodlebug' was passing over towards some other unfortunate; if it cut out, you got

130 Bombs dropped from low-flying aircraft often bounced. One landed on Longland Road and exploded in Victoria Drive 200 yards away. Here a bomb has passed through a house in Waterworks Road to explode on the cottages at the back.

131 A 'Doodlebug' (V1) flying over Birling Gap and the Seven Sisters just west of Eastbourne 1944. It was named after a midget racing car popular in the 1930s which had the same sound.

down, for there would be an explosion within a few seconds: a worrying moment. Laurence Snowball commented, 'It was thanks to the bravery of all the D-Day troops that Eastbourne was saved from prolonged V1 bombardment. One of the most remarkable features of everyday life was the wonderful spirit. If a family was bombed-out they would receive offers of accommodation, clothes and food, often from people quite unknown to them. We could do with some of this spirit all the time without the bombs.' In October, as a gesture of reconciliation, the Rt Rev. George Bell, Bishop of Chichester, dedicated the murals of German-born artist, Hans Feibusch, in war-damaged St Elisabeth's Church. There was much discussion about whether Glenn Miller, the American band leader, had died off Beachy Head on 15 December 1944. He was flying to Paris in a Norseman when 138 Lancaster bombers, returning from an aborted raid, jettisoned their bombs into the Channel and reported that an explosion was seen below. Conversely, the Dresden bombing by the

132 Most of the V1s landed harmlessly on the Downs, and two actually struck the cliff face of Beachy Head. On 21 June and 1 August 1944 fighters shot down V1s over empty countryside, but occasionally things went wrong, and on 4 July a fighter pilot shot down a V1 and misjudged the fall. It missed the open country by a few yards to fall behind Astaire Avenue: six houses were demolished and over 30 people injured.

133 The bombed site of Caffyn's Garage in Marine Parade, with RAF petrol tankers awaiting service in the repair shop at Leeds Avenue. Of 450 Caffyn's staff at the beginning of the war, 370 served in the forces and 24 won awards. Sydney Caffyn, grandson of the founder, led a unit of the Home Guard and, despite destruction of many of the workshops, kept up the company's war effort. Edward, his brother, was involved in the formation of REME, and finished the war a brigadier with the personal thanks of Field-Marshal Bernard Montgomery.

USAF and RAF was hardly given a thought. One who went through the war in Eastbourne said, 'I have no hatred for the Germans, but they deserved all they got. One of the hopes that kept us going in 1940 was that eventually they would be given as much as, if not more, than what they threw at us. Don't forget the war wasn't over in February 1945 – Anne Frank was yet to die in Belsen and the last V2 rocket wasn't till March.' Some of the restrictions were, however, being eased and the ending of the blackout was an especially joyful moment.

At the outbreak of war Eastbourne had awaited 20,000 evacuees with trepidation. In February 1945 the town greeted 10,000 repatriated Australian prisoners-of-war who were billeted around the town, or in some instances admitted to St Mary's Hospital, while they waited to board ships for home. Mrs Florence Tomsett and Mrs Doris Pumfrey were among the Red Cross members who lent a hand: 'We visited some of the lads in hospital, taking toiletries to them and writing letters if they weren't well enough themselves.' The Aussies were given a great welcome, and not just because they had oodles of chocolate, which was on ration for the civilians; they also helped renovate the Saffrons' county cricket pitch after five years of neglect and at least one bomb on the square. After helping to celebrate VE Day and a Grand Thank You Garden Party for the town on 6 July 1945, they were soon on their way.

Black Friday, 13 September 1940, came back to haunt the town. One UXB that had fallen on the Seaside recreation ground that day had penetrated so deeply it had been left and, by custom, given a nickname. On 3 January 1946 'Hermann' was dug out from seven yards down, with the BBC broadcasting the big bang. The war left other scars, and the last bomb site wasn't built over until the 1980s; in 2001 an estate agent estimated that 10 per cent of Eastbourne's buildings had evidence of war damage. Thornton Court, in Bourne Street, was built on the site of 139 'Bomb Alley' damaged properties, and in 1952 a wall plaque was unveiled which read, '...erected by Eastbourne Corporation as a tribute to the fortitude shown by the inhabitants of the town during the air raids of the war of 1939-45 ...' The siren went 1,346 times, there were 353 local warnings, and about 500 episodes without warning. The raids resulted in 174 civilian deaths, 443 seriously hurt, and 489 other injuries. Casualties also occurred among the local troops. After the First World War the Commonwealth War Graves Commission developed a pantograph machine for roughing out unit badges on the headstones; in 1945 the Commission found one of these machines while searching in an Eastbourne builder's yard and it was copied for the new headstones.

Six

Spotlight on a Changing Town

'When in 1946 I first came to Eastbourne,' says Betty Cobb, 'I was struck by the extent of the damage.' The demand for housing was acute in the town where some 500 houses had been destroyed, 1,000 made uninhabitable, and ten times that number damaged.[1] The housing problems were met by renting all sorts of accommodation, by repairing war-damaged property and, thirdly, by 'pre-fabs', single-storey 12 yards by eight yards prefabricated houses of aluminium and asbestos/cement which had a refrigerator too. The first foundations were dug by German prisoners-of-war.

An early reopening of hotels and other parts of the holiday scene was vital to provide employment and for Eastbourne to regain its reputation as a leading holiday town. George Hill, who became the Entertainments and Catering Manager in 1946, was an able man who provided the energy and

hard work to promote the town and maintain it as a top resort. With his intimate knowledge of the theatre he unerringly picked successful shows.

The *Grand Hotel*, used by the RAF during the war, reopened in September 1946. It has had a number of changes of ownership over the years but remains Eastbourne's top hotel. The pier had suffered badly. A water tank, hit by enemy fire, had swamped the theatre below, the seats and curtains had been removed for a garrison theatre at Newhaven, and a mine exploded near the shore end, damaging the old music pavilion. The infamous gap was bridged by concrete slabs, and by 1946 the pier opened again with the music pavilion converted for ballroom dancing, which was popular in the 1940s and '50s. The theatre reopened and after 1948 was dominated by the *Starlight* summer show, built around the personality of Sandy Powell, whose

134 A public meeting decided that Eastbourne's war memorial should be houses for the war disabled and a Book of Remembrance kept at the Town Hall. War Memorial Houses, Victoria Drive were furnished in 1952 at a cost of £17,405. Over time many improvements have been added: gas central heating in 1969, porches in 1982, and special fittings such as hoists and chair lifts.

135 Eastbourne's crowded front in the 1950s. After the glorious summer of 1947, and throughout the 1950s, hotels, boarding houses, theatres and the pier were packed out, and all the holiday businesses did well in the season.

company did 15 seasons in a row to 1970. One of the last of the music hall comedians, his catchphrase 'Can you hear me mother?' was born during a broadcast when he dropped his script and, bending down for it, muttered the words. He and his wife, Kay, lived in Elms Avenue, where they ran a boarding house when 'resting'.

Only eight private schools returned after the war, and since then Ascham, Chelmsford Hall, Neville House and Beresford House have also closed, leaving St Andrew's, St Bede's, Eastbourne College (all co-educational) and Moira House. To some extent the loss of the schools was relieved by the Schools of English for foreigners which have flourished in the town since the 1950s. Examples are the Eastbourne School of English, the English Centre and the ABC Language School. Providing

lodging for the students gives an extra stimulus to the economy.

For a couple of years from 1947 there was a Teachers' Training College, mainly for demobbed troops, housed in adapted ex-schools such as Queenwood in Darley Road. Technical skills would be needed to rebuild, but Eastbourne had no Technical College after the 1942 bombing. Incredibly, there was an immediate offer of three rooms by the commander of Princess Pat's Regiment at The Grange, a private school in St Anne's Road closed since 1940. When the regiment moved out the Technical College took over what became the site of the Eastbourne College of Arts and Technology for the next 50 years. All the rooms were brought into use, with an engineering work-shop, a chemistry laboratory and drawing office

136 Since 1954 Compton Place, Eastbourne's only Grade I listed building, has housed an LTC College, but Andrew, 11th Duke of Devonshire (1920-) still plays an active part in the town.

fitted in somehow. The hall on the ground floor was used for assembly, a gym, a dining room and a music room. Conditions were basic: 'downstairs there was a pneumonia alley' and, upstairs, a 'pleurisy passage', and 'winter absences were frequent'.[2]

The catering department was the first to move to purpose-built accommodation at the King's Drive site, followed by the School of Art, and from 1997 all ECAT departments were at South Downs College, Cross Levels Way. The St Anne's Road and Selwyn Road sites and Eversley Court were sold for housing.

The late 1940s and the 1950s turned out to be happy times for the holiday industry. Brian Allchorn, who joined the family pleasure-boat business with his brother Colin in 1951, says, 'There was a boom after the war. A trip round the lighthouse left every

half-an-hour, and you would manage ten trips a day at the height of summer. We didn't have to keep a record before the *Marchioness* disaster, but must have carried near 50,000 over the season.'

Cecil Johnson cashed in, starting *Fun in the Air* at the Redoubt Music Garden in 1947 and, in 1949, bringing the review *By the Way* to the Winter Garden. The Corporation transport department got in on the act by slicing the top off five buses and painting them white to use as open-top buses - having given each a name so that children would insist on using all five.

To the great benefit of the town's employment situation, the Dental Estimates Board (now Dental Practice Board) opened in 1948 on the Temple Grove School site in Compton Place Road. Its function was to check all the NHS dental returns.

137 A bird's-eye view of the Birds Eye factory in Lottbridge Drove in about 1975. It was the largest factory on the estate, profitably turning out millions of frozen food products, but rationalisation determined its closure, which commenced in 1983. The site is now Tesco's Superstore, which moved from the Langney Shopping Centre, Eastbourne's first.

It provided clerical employment for about 1,000 people until computerisation and was a most enlightened employer, giving opportunities to part-time and disabled staff.

For local farmers things were looking up too. Betty Turner says, 'The war had brought guaranteed prices when it was the Ministry who decided the crop you sowed however unsuitable the ground. Most farmers dealt in cash and guarded their money, but by 1949 good money had been splashed out on a Hayter grass cutter, and enterprising farmers had invested £350 on a grey Ferguson petrol tractor.' A 1948 outbreak of food poisoning was allegedly traced to the high-class Scotch Bakery cream.

The 1951 population of 57,801 was fewer than in 1921, whereas Blackpool and Bournemouth, which had been smaller in 1881, were now three times Eastbourne's size.

Between the wars Compton Place had been used mainly for children of the Cavendish family to convalesce after childhood illnesses, but Edward, 10th Duke of Devonshire enjoyed visiting Eastbourne. In November 1950 he decided to take down a tree behind the house and died of a heart attack, at 55, just before various tax-avoidance schemes were implemented, and the death duties came to £4.7m, with interest at £1,000 a day. The Eastbourne ground rents (the *Royal*'s lease is now about £90,000 a year) and the Derbyshire mineral rights were the only profitable parts of the estates, but the Duke and Duchess dealt energetically with the situation and the final debts were paid within 16 years.

As part of the Council's commitment towards looking after their infirm elderly residents, Trevin Towers opened in 1951 as a residential home. The educational services had to cope not only with the repair and replacement of damaged schools, but with the increase in numbers of schoolchildren from about 5,700 in 1950 to 6,700 ten years later. Highfield County Primary School in Hampden Park was the first new school, followed rapidly by Motcombe in 1951, Roselands Infants in 1952, and Langney Primary in 1955; St Mary's Infants was replaced by Pashley Down.

Antibiotics were revolutionising the treatment of infections. Streptomycin in 1952 ensured the first survival of a patient with TB meningitis at St Mary's Hospital - and she was still going strong towards the end of the century. St Mary's Hospital had better facilities than the Maternity Home for Caesarean deliveries and blood transfusions and from the mid-1950s to 1976 most of Eastbourne's babies were born there.

The Eastbourne Rugby Club prospered after the war. It had joined the County Rugby Union in 1895, and by 1934 was playing along King's Drive; there was a stand there from 1938. In 1969 a new building was opened on the Park Avenue frontage.

The 1953 Coronation had a dramatic effect on a drab country not yet recovered from rationing, bomb sites and austerity. For a tremendous number of people it was their first television programme. The year was also marked by the golden jubilee of the Girls' High School. The next year the Eastbourne Association of Sussex Folk was founded and new cars became available from stock for the first time since the war, resulting in record profits for Caffyn's. Building restrictions were lifted that year and construction of business premises allowed, so Eastbourne's gaps began to be filled. In the 1950s the Park Gates site was rebuilt, and Grand Court and Metropole Court replaced hotels. Noteworthy replacements were the Terminus Road Barclays Bank in 1958 and, in 1966, the east wing of the *Cavendish Hotel*.[3]

The Council took the first steps towards an industrial park when Armour & Co., a subsidiary of an American pharmaceutical company, established a factory of some 30,000 sq. ft., with 250 employees, on the Brampton Road Trading Estate in 1954. It was a pleasant, clean business, and proved to be the catalyst which stimulated other companies to come to the town. Such a measure was not welcomed by

all, the hotel trade complaining that light industry would deprive them of cheap female labour during the holiday season, but it was a success and was joined by similar ventures. The Council took steps to develop provision for light industry, and Lottbridge Drove opened for traffic in 1964, Winscombe Farm being bulldozed to make room for the developments.

Over the years businesses have come and gone. Stainless Steel Pumps has been there for years, and Nobo plc in Lottbridge Drove, which produces office equipment, was a local firm until taken over in 1997. Eastbourne Car Auctions moved from the centre of Eastbourne; others, such as Hotchkiss, moved away altogether. Queensway Furniture Store in Edison Road was empty for five years before being sold to the Kings Church in 1996. Eastbourne has always been perceived as a rich town so development grants have been sparse.

Holidays abroad were rare after the war, and in 1946 each person was only allowed to take £25 out of the country. The first coach tour from Eastbourne was in 1950, and until 1952 coaches had to be loaded by crane at Dover. When overseas holidays took off in the 1960s the new local industries helped cushion the loss of trade, and hotels relied more on the conference trade, product launches, and 'Golden Oldies', especially out of season. The 'Crumbles Tramway' ran from Royal Parade past Princes Park to the Crumbles between 1954 and 1969.[4] It could be said that it was replaced by the ubiquitous Dotto train, which started in Eastbourne in 1988.

The Redoubt Model Village, designed and built by Benjamin White, was a work of inspiration and high craftsmanship. The dry moat of the Redoubt had been terraced over when the Music Garden was built and the resultant 'cave' became another of Ben White's ventures when, in 1961, he opened the Blue Temple Grotto and Aquarium.[5]

Uncle Bertie's Hour, featuring conjuring, ventriloquism, fancy dress parades and talent contests, at the Redoubt Music Garden attracted the crowds throughout the summer from 1949 to 1963. Uncle Bertie, Bertram Otto, also built model railways.[6] The ruins of St Anne's Church in Upperton Gardens were demolished for housing in 1955, but a piece of masonry was used as a foundation stone of St

138   The Crumbles Tramway opened officially at Whitsun 1955. The 2ft.-gauge track was half a mile long, and the vehicles were powered from overhead electric lines. Fares ranged from 2d. to 10d. It was a much-loved feature and the owners wanted to extend further but the Council had new housing developments in mind. The tramway moved to Seaton, Devon at the end of the 1969 season.

139   The model village at the Redoubt. The site opened to the public in 1957 and soon became a major attraction. Two visitors are looking over Kingston Agnes Manor, one of five sections in the display, where most of the models were exact scale replicas of actual buildings. Casemates of the Redoubt can be seen in the background.

140 The *Germania* stranded at the foot of Beachy Head in April 1955. She had been in a collision in the Channel and grounded off Cow Gap. This was the last time a breeches-buoy was fired off Beachy Head, although it was not used in the rescue. The ship was eventually towed to Bremen. Notice remnants of radar installations on the cliff top.

Richard's, Langney in 1957. The same year St John the Evangelist Church in Meads was rebuilt with help from the War Damage Commission. Lady Gillman, who dedicated the plaque, was the daughter of Mr and Mrs Charles Rube, who paid for much of the work. The tower was all that remained of the former church, and its ground floor was converted into a chapel in memory of all those who gave their lives for the cause of freedom in two world wars. Marks & Spencer had opened a temporary store in 1943, on the other side of Terminus Road, until a replacement could be erected on the old site in 1955. The new store was to undergo enlargement and conversion of the first floor to shopping space.

In 1956 Dr Bodkin Adams, a local general practitioner, was accused of the murder of three patients, although the press declared there were 400 victims, and he was tried in a celebrated case

141 On Saturday 4 June 1955 the Duke of Edinburgh came to Eastbourne for the Silver Jubilee conference of the Royal Air Forces Association. When a Sunderland flying boat, coming in for an air show, misjudged the landing it sank just off the beach; one airman was killed and three were injured.

142 Frederick Soddy FRS (1877-1956). Born in Bolton Road, Soddy attended Eastbourne College and Merton College and graduated with first class honours in Chemistry. As Professor of Chemistry at Oxford he collaborated with Rutherford and Ramsay, and coined the term 'isotope' for different forms of the same element. In 1921 he was the first Oxford graduate to receive a Nobel Prize. There is a tablet outside 6 Bolton Road and at Eastbourne College.

143 Dr Bodkin Adams (second from right) at a function with Norah O'Hara (sitting second from left), to whom he was engaged at one time. The dramatic nature of his trial for murdering a patient propelled his counsel, Geoffrey Lawrence, into the limelight, and influenced the Criminal Justice Act of 1967. It set a case law that treatment inadvertently causing death was not murder, and led to changes in the Drug Regulations. Speculation continues as to whether he was a murderer or just greedy and disorganised.

at the Old Bailey.[7] Rumours about the 'Eastbourne Bluebeard' spread from the town to the country and all over the world. In Paul Harris' words, this was 'The best publicity the town could have had, very good for business'. The town was prospering. Louis G. Ford's more than doubled their turnover in the 1950s, even though the Suez Crisis of 1956 brought Territorial activity to the Ordnance Yard in Seaside, along with petrol rationing and credit restrictions.

Miss Randall was 60 in 1945, but by now girls were wanting a career in catering, so she carried on and the school, later college, was extended from 1 to 11 Silverdale Road with hostels in Jevington Gardens and South Cliff. By now her girls could be out till midnight, although Eastbourne College boys were known to climb the drainpipes in the early hours. At the golden jubilee in 1957 Ranny was presented with a mink jacket and a wedding cake, which she said she had always wanted. She died in May 1959. The college closed in 1996.

In 1957 Harold Wenham of the Eastbourne Round Table revived the pre-war Carnival, with Roy Forster, Tony Hudson and John Claremont. They staged a Fun Fair at Seaside Recreation Ground, a dance to choose the Carnival Queen, and a procession of 100 floats along the front. From 1961 the event was arranged by Trustees, including Mayor Percy Wood and Paul Harris. In 1970 the Eastbourne Lions Club took over and ran it until 1998.

All Saints' Hospital had been a military hospital again in the war. Although its work resumed in 1945, by 1959 the few nursing sisters found they could no longer continue their service. Instead of being sold for a development of 41 houses, the hospital was taken over by the NHS.[8]

Plans to build the new Congress Theatre adjacent to the Devonshire Park Winter Garden, with a connecting restaurant, were agreed in 1956, and the opening by Princess Margaret in 1963 was in the presence of Dame Flora Robson and Sir Arthur Bliss. It was sorely needed and an asset, but the restaurant was not big enough and it has had acoustic and ventilation problems.

Before 1952 Sainsbury's shop assistants added up the prices and pound notes had to be changed by the cashier. The Terminus Road store was altered to supermarket style that year and mechanical tills

144 On Monday 25 August 1958, at 7.28a.m., on a pouring wet day, a steam-hauled train from Glasgow passed signals at danger and ran into a waiting electric train at Eastbourne. Five persons were killed instantly, including the driver of the local train. The walking wounded were taken to St Mary's Hospital and 23 seriously injured casualties went to the Princess Alice. One died that day, but the rest made good progress. One traveller who escaped uninjured had the dreadful experience of having to climb over one of the victims to escape from the wreckage; British Rail awarded him £10 to clean his suit.

introduced, but they were hard work until the advent of the electric till in 1960. Eastbourne's Crematorium at Hide Hollow, Langney opened in 1960, and the YM/YWCA, previously in Langney Road and at 5 Bolton Road, moved to Ocklynge in the 1960s.

In 1960 the Redoubt was declared an Ancient Monument and in 1973, when Peter Bedford was Director of Combined Entertainments, the Council took over the Model Village and Aquarium. A £100,000 program of renovation commenced under the Curator, David Galer. In order to pave over the Redoubt parade ground parts of the Model

Village were removed, and in 1977 the remaining buildings were reduced to rubble.[9] The Marquess of Abergavenny officially opened the Redoubt, restored to its original condition, on 18 May 1979, and it is now used as the Sussex Combined Services Museum and for exhibitions, concerts and firework displays.[10]

In March 1960 Katie Juliette Underhay, a local councillor, put plans before the Council to pull down Hillcote, the school converted into flats, and build in its place a tower block of high-class flats some 200ft. (70m.) high; it is said two more towers were to follow. After a storm of protest the height

145 The Wish Tower Café and Sun Lounge was provided by Gilbert Samuel Foyle in 1961 as a tribute to the town's fortitude during the Blitz. Foyle (1886-1971), a founder of the bookshop, lived in Burlington Place and was a member of Eastbourne Council from 1952 to 1962. Another benefaction in 1957 enabled the Council to buy 94 acres of the Downs near Whitbread Hollow, and a path there is named Foyle Way. The Wish Tower had been designated a scheduled monument, renovated and was open to the public as a museum and for puppet shows. The present gun, a 68-pounder, is not original, having been cast in 1858.

146 The Indian Pavilion (above), or Devonshire Lawns Restaurant, was demolished in 1961 to make way for the Congress Theatre (right). It is shown here just before opening in 1963. In 1955 the Council had contemplated building a new conference and concert hall in place of the Wish Tower, and then threatened to knock down the Tower for a café.

147 Eastbourne front from Foyle Way, showing not just the chalk Pinnacle, the Parades, Wish Tower and the pier, but South Cliff Tower. It is a most desirable residence in a lovely part of the town, and Cllr Mrs Underhay had an apartment on the 13th floor, but most folk considered it quite out of place, intrusive from every view and blocking the scene for much of South Cliff.

of the building was restricted to 200ft., but South Cliff Tower went ahead in 1966, the year of Katie's mayoralty. The town was appalled and determined that 'Katie's Folly' should not be repeated. Perhaps, rather like Peacehaven, its presence curtailed other outgrowths. One result was the formation of what is now the Eastbourne Society, with the aim of vetting such planning applications; another was that Katie was thrown off the Council, even though it was the convention for the retiring mayor to be unopposed. Mrs M.W. Rice-Pyle trounced her at the polls.

Pococks Farm was demolished for development of the Rodmill estate in the winter of 1962/3. The farm was believed to be the old 15th-century Manor House of Beverington. Architects had advised against houses on the shingle to the east, but newer building techniques meant that in 1971 over 1,800 houses would be under construction, mainly in Langney.

The town's first traffic wardens quietly took up their duties on 1 April 1964, although Eastbourne has resisted the allure of parking meters. The Borough Council bought the Royal Hippodrome, Seaside Road in 1962 after leasing it for five years. Formerly the Theatre Royal, it was one of the first theatres to have a concrete fire escape. In the 1970s Jack Tripp and Walter Landauer were popular

148 The Sussex Club (now Clive Court), where the Central Library was temporarily housed from 1946 to 1964. The official opening of the new Central Library was by Sir Frank Francis. In its first year of operation over a million books were issued. Coin-operated photocopiers and microfilm reader-printers have been introduced since, along with fax machines, CDs, PC access and automated on-line book issue systems.

149   Eastbourne's Carpet Gardens. The town's floral displays are renowned and the town has won many Britain in Bloom awards. These seafront gardens are famous the world over, but there are many others around the town.

performers there. From 1946 the Central Library had been in temporary accommodation in the Sussex Club, now Clive Court, on the front. The conditions were not ideal and all welcomed the new library on 6 April 1964, whose first book was issued to Mayor Bernard Raven. The Llewellyn-build is steel-framed and finished in Portland stone with some Lakeland Green slate. The sculpture on the south side represents 'A Scholar Seeking Knowledge' by Hammond Davis. The cost was £143,743, and £193,611 for the adjoining Council Office block, of which the War Damage Commission contributed £130,523.

Confectioners before and after the war included the Scotch Bakery and Baker Sons & Hyde. Bondolfi's of Cornfield Terrace, who had been in Eastbourne since 1895 when the family came from Italy, was the place to meet. Says director Alex Bransgrove, 'We processed 1¼ ton of chocolate a month.' In the 1960s Chez Maurice, the town's

first bistro, arrived. In 1965, on the centenary of William Caffyn's first shop, the company celebrated with the opening of award-winning premises in Upperton Road. By now the company had a turnover of over £10m., a staff of some 1,500, and the fourth generation of Alan, Anthony and Robert Caffyn had joined the firm. Sir Sydney was mayor from 1956 to 1958 and 1973 to 1974, Chancellor of Sussex University and a Freeman of the Borough, and Lady Annie was renowned for her good works.

Eastbourne United Football Club achieved fame through its managers. Harry Haslam and Gordon Jago went on to top clubs, while Ron Greenwood became the England manager. An important step to ensure healthy conditions for bathers at Eastbourne was the construction in 1965 of a new sewage outfall, with an underground pumping station near Langney Point. Further measures were taken in 1997 and 2001 to comply with EU regulations.

Having survived incendiary bombs, *Beachy Head Hotel* burnt down on 6 April 1966. Firefighter Albert Green explained, 'It is in a vulnerable position. The wind fans the flames, and we had to ferry water up to the site, which meant the engines doing a relay and coming back with 400 gallons.' It was rebuilt and popular for Rotary functions and Sunday lunches until burnt down again in 1994, although it was replaced within the year. The 300 staff of the telephone exchange at Upperton Road coped with the town's calls until June 1966, when the town was converted to automatic dialling, although 'trunk' calls remained. In 1971 a cordless switchroom opened at Selwyn Road and the HPO room closed. By 1977 there were over 15,000 Eastbourne subscribers, with another 30,000 outside the Borough.

Bradford's had absorbed Knight's and, in 1958, been one of the first coal merchants to sell pre-packed paper sacks, 'A boon for people living in flats'; but North Sea gas and inflated costs quickened the trend to larger businesses and in 1971 Bradford's merged with Corrall's. The local dairies also amalgamated in 1959, and are now Unigate. The Eastbourne Pier Company sold out in 1968/9 to Trust House (later Forte). The pier had a narrow squeak in 1963, when a merchant ship almost collided with it after catching fire off Beachy Head. Seven years later an employee of three weeks standing, 'a carpenter with a chip', had another try and set fire to the Pier Theatre. Most of it was saved, but access to the camera obscura was destroyed and has not been replaced.

On Sunday afternoon, 20 October 1968, the tanker *Sitakund* suffered a series of explosions in the Channel, which shook the town's doors and windows, and came to rest off Holywell. Despite fatalities among the ship's crew, and further explosions and fires, the lifeboat under Coxswain Derek Huggett stood by while the Fire Brigade successfully dealt with the flames. Part of the ship was towed away in 1969 and the rest demolished by explosive in 1972.

The pedestrian precinct in Terminus Road was introduced experimentally at the start of the 1970s, and on 7 October 1970 the Winifred Lee Health Centre in Wartling Road, Eastbourne's first purpose-built Health Centre, was opened. The

150 Since the 1960s the old houses along Upperton Road have been replaced by somewhat overpowering blocks of flats. In the 1880s a house called Braemar was built as part of a development of fine private houses along Upperton Road. By the late 1990s it was *Brownings Hotel* and housed asylum seekers. When it was knocked down, in 2001, the nearby *Cedars* was the sole survivor of the 19th century.

151 The 'Corporation of Eastbourne', 1995-6. Mayor and Mayoress Ron and Elsie Parsons are left centre, with Leslie and Doreen Mason their deputies.

Sussex Police Authority was formed in 1968 and Eastbourne lost its police force. The Fire Brigade had been returned from the National Fire Service to Eastbourne control in 1948, all the pre-war appliances had been replaced by 1954, and in December 1973 the Duke of Norfolk opened the new Fire Station in Whitley Road, but it was lost following local government reorganisation in 1974. Education, Libraries, Planning, Refuse Disposal,

Social Services and Transport were also taken over by the County Council, significantly reducing Eastbourne's importance. A closure that year was the Bell Hostel in Salehurst Road. Founded by Mrs Bell in 1886, the Upwick Vale Rescue Home was for 'fallen women', or unmarried mothers.

Over the dry, hot summer of 1976 surgical and some other units moved to the new District General Hospital at Kings Drive which was officially opened the next year by Princess Alexandra. The Devonshire Baths were used less since many schools had not returned to the town, and others built their own pools. In 1970 the tower containing the water tanks was declared unsafe and demolished; flooding in 1975 caused further deterioration, and the baths closed at the end of 1976, with the staff transferred to the new Sovereign Pool in 1977.

St Peter's Church, Meads was suddenly knocked down in 1972 and Redman King House is now on the site. Before demolition of the Jesus House site for St Mary's Court, a residential home, Lawrence Stevens conducted an excavation in 1977-8.

Eastbourne's Arndale Centre officially opened its doors on 7 October 1980 and transformed local shopping habits. Apart from being detrimental to the shops in Seaside Road and Grove Road, which are only just recovering, the all-in-one-place shopping has proved popular, although there is doubt about whether the mix of shops is right for the town, and few community facilities are provided.

152 Many organisations created their own war memorials to old boys or employees. This war memorial arch in Meads to '49 valiant men' is all that is left of Ascham St Vincent Prep. School, taken over by Eastbourne College after the Second World War and closed in 1977. The school was demolished in 1984 for Ascham Close and Vincent Close, seen behind the archway.

153 The junction of Cornfield and Terminus Roads, before and after the Arndale Centre was opened in 1981. The name comes from the founders of a Property Trust: Arnold Hagenbach and Sam Chippendale. The centre has had a second phase added, and a facelift and £4m. refurbishment in 1997 gave natural light to the walkways.

154   Over the summer of 1981 Arthur Lowe paid his last visit to the Devonshire Park Theatre. The theatre, along with the old racquets court, was bought by the Council in February 1957 for £33,750, after being leased for five years.

Sainsbury's, there from the start, adopted computerised checkouts from 1988, Sunday trading after 1992 and built Cross Levels Way to their superstore. From the Terminus Road precinct you can still see Sussex Gardens, an early terrace of private houses now incorporated into the shops, and observe the stone urns on the roof line.

The Star Brewery, in Old Town from 1777, ceased brewing in 1965, but a development scheme was turned down in 1969. The site was eventually sold to Tesco's in 1979 but two years later they sold to Safeway, who started building in November 1983. The following year the widening of nearby Church Street, first mooted before 1914, finally got under way. Once completed, Ocklynge Road, one of the town's oldest thoroughfares, no longer had traffic access into Church Street. Woolworth's superstore

in Terminus Road closed in September 1984 after 60 years of trading. As part of the town's centenary commemorations in 1983, a Local History Museum was opened in the Towner Art Gallery building. It is well worth a visit.

A marina had been discussed in 1962, when BP tentatively agreed to put up £250,000. The first Parliamentary Bill for a harbour on the Crumbles was, however, defeated in 1975, but approval was received in 1980, whereupon Tarmac Construction and Asda bought land from the Chatsworth Trustees. Hall Aggregates, extractors of gravel from the site since 1931, with an output of 250,000 tons a year, closed their plant in 1986. The project consisted of an outer tidal harbour, inner marina, berths for some 2,000 vessels, and residential and business development. Work

155 Princess Diana opened the Sovereign Centre in Royal Parade in June 1989. A new swimming pool had opened near Prince's Park in 1977, and the Sovereign Harbour was under construction at the time. The Sovereign Centre was revamped in 2000.

saw the first boat through the lock gates. Now the 365-acre Sovereign Harbour, with 65 acres of water, stretches from Langney to Pevensey Bay, and provides good quality, well-spaced houses. The *Duke of Kent* lifeboat was launched from the fishing station slipway for the last time on 20 May 1993 and the lifeboat moved to the outer harbour of the marina. In 1994 a new lifeboat station was built near the lock gates. A few fishermen's huts remain on the front.

The marina, shopping centres and housing estates have removed the scars of war, and there are now some thirty local authority schools, from Bishop Bell in Priory Road to Willingdon Trees in Magnolia Drive. A few new churches have been built, but more have been demolished or converted. Christ Church still has its Willis organ, the only one on the south coast, but the modern congregation speaks 26 languages. Theatres have their good and bad years.[11] Tourism remains important for employment but is now well supported by light industry, mainly along Lottbridge Drive. By 2000 Eastbourne was becoming a short-break resort, but the hotels were

commenced in 1991, granite being brought from Norway for the harbour arms. On 19 February 1993 the barrier between the sea and the outer harbour at the Sovereign Marina was breached, allowing the tides to flood in and out, and May

156 The Devonshire Park Women's Championships of 1994, the year after the North Stand burnt down. It was replaced by three up-to-date stands with a total seating capacity of 7,500 and better facilities. The Park's first tennis tournament was in 1881. Martina Navratilova won the title 11 times.

157 In 1991 the Eastbourne Society and the Friends of the Towner restored the near-derelict 18th-century hermitage in the Manor Gardens. 'Moorish' decorations under the circular thatched roof, enchanting ogee-shaped sash windows and Adam-style interior decoration in Wedgewood blue make this an architectural gem.

full during the special attractions, such as the Devonshire Park tennis tournament.[12] The most recent royal visitor is Prince Charles, who opened an Age Concern Centre on 20 November 2000.

Eastbourne was delighted to hear that Andrew, 11th Duke of Devonshire is to become an honorary Freeman of the Borough in recognition of his family's rôle as a major landowner in the town, and his own continued interest.[13] The attractive seafront has no shops along its three miles, in part thanks to restrictive covenants enforced by the Dukes of Devonshire.

There is no doubt that Eastbourne Past has shaped Eastbourne Present, and there is much to be proud of: ex-mayor Ron Parsons believes 'Eastbourne is a glorious place'; but there are lessons to be learnt for the benefit of Eastbourne Future.

158 'Airbourne' is the name for the aircraft display held annually along the front in the 1990s. It is often combined with the Red Arrows and a car exhibition, and 250,000 pour into the town for the occasion.

Notes and References

One The New Resort 1780-1850, pp.1-18
1. *The Book of Eastbourne*, ed. Budgen, W., Willoughby, W.G., 1931.
2. Royer, J., *Eastbourne being a descriptive account of that village in the county of Sussex and its environs*, 1787.
3. Lewis, M., 'Visit of the Royal children', *Eastbourne Local History Society Newsletter* [ELHS NL] 60, 1986, 20-6.
4. Chambers, G.F., *Eastbourne Memories*, 1910.
5. *Eastbourne Gazette* 31/8/1864.
6. Brockhurst, E., *The Gables*, ELHS NL 64, 1987, 21-3. Cooper, R., *Reminiscences of Eastbourne*, 1903.
7. *Census of 1841 Eastbourne* (intro. Hodsoll, V.) ELHS 1990.
8. Hudson, A., 'Gazetteer of Barracks in Sussex (1793-1815)', *Sussex Archaeological Society* [SAS] 1986; PRO WO 40/7 July 1794.
9. Gilbert, R., *Eastbourne prepares to meet Old Boney*, 1980.
10. *Sussex County Magazine*, 9, 1936, 436.
11. Sutcliffe, S., *Martello Towers*, 1972. Spears, H.D., *Local Martello Towers*, 1974.
12. Spears, H., *The Redoubt Eastbourne*, 1976.
13. Douch, J., *Smuggling*, 1985; Milton, F.R., *The Fight Against Smuggling around Eastbourne and Newhaven*, 1991; Waugh, M., *Smuggling in Kent and Sussex 1700-1840*, 1985, Webb, W., *Coastguard*, 1976.
14. Brandon, P., Short, B., *South East England since AD 1000*, 1990.
15. Minutes of Eastbourne Union Guardians, East Sussex PRO [ESPRO] ref. G13/1a/1 & G13/8/1.
16. *Ibid.* 11/12/1835, 18/12/1835.
17. *Ibid.* 3/7/1835.
18. Chapman's Stage-Coach between Eastbourne and Brighton only made its last run in 1905.
19. The word 'Downs' is said by Lower, M.A., *A History of Sussex*, 1870, to come from the Anglo-Saxon 'Dun' for a hill.
20. Claremont, J.V.C., *A History of the Eastbourne Law Society*, 1998; the town was trying to establish that a foreigner did not gain residence by occupying a settlement for 40 days.

Two Before The Royal Princes, pp.19-34
1. Drewett, P., Rudling, D., Gardiner M., *The South East to AD 1000*, 1988.
2. Stevens, L., *Shinewater Bronze Age Settlement*, 1997.
3. Tabor, J., 'Eastbourne Roman Villa' in *Philosophical Trans.* quoted *Sussex Archaeological Collections* [SAC 14] 1862, 126. Stevens, L., Gilbert, R., *The Eastbourne Roman Villa*, 1973. Sutton, T., *The Eastbourne Roman Villa*, SAC 90, 1951-2, 1-4.
4. Drewett, P., *The Archaeology of Bullock Down*, SAS 1982.
5. British Library MS, 15776: ff. 213.
6. Bland, R.F., 'The 1973 Beachy Head Treasure Trove of Third Century Antoniniani', *Numismatic Chronicle*, 1979; (7) 19: 61-107. Budgen, W., 'A Hoard of Roman Coins', SAC 58, 1916, 193-4. Calvert, T., 'Short Notice of a Find of Roman Coins near Eastbourne', SAC N&Q 31, 1881, 201-5. Carson, R.A.G., 'Beachy Head Treasure Trove of Roman Imperial Silver Coins', *Numismatic Chronicle* 1968; (7) VIII: 67-81. Dolley, R.H.M., O'Donovan, M.A., 'The 1961 Beachy Head (Bullock Down) Hoard of Third Century Coins of the Central and Gallic Empires', Numismatic Chronicle 1962; (7) II: 163-188. Haverfield, F., 'On a Hoard of Roman Coins Found near Eastbourne in 1899', SAC 1901; 44: 1-8.
7. Horsfield, T.W., *History, Antiquities and Topography of the County of Sussex*, 1835.
8. *Domesday Book Sussex* ed. Morris, J., 1976.
9. *The Book of Eastbourne,* ed. Budgen, W., Willoughby, W.G., 1931.

10. Camden, W., *Britannia*, 1607, 2 edn. 1806, ed. Gough, R, 271.

11. Spears, H.D., *Flint Buildings in and around Eastbourne*, 1986.

12. Blencowe, R.W., 'Paxhill and its neighbourhood', SAC 11, 1859, 33-4.

13. Beckett, A., 'The Battle of Beachy Head', *Sussex County Magazine*, 3, 1929, 378. Mordal, J., *Twenty-five centuries of Sea Warfare*, 1959. Sanderson, M., *Sea Battles*, 1975. Stevens, L., 'The Battle of Beachy Head', ELHS NL 77, 1990, 13-15.

14. Budgen, W., *Old Eastbourne*, 1912.

15. Elleray, D.R., *Eastbourne A Pictorial History*, 1978. The Greys was sometimes spelt Grays.

16. Macky, J., *A Journey through England*, Letter VI London: Caldecott 1714.

17. Thomas Willard was Spencer Compton's election agent in 1715. After paying a bill of £13 at the *Lamb* he wrote, 'the voters drank your health, but parted with no money'.

18. Cartwright, J.J., *The travels through England of Dr. Richard Pococke*, 1889, Camden Society 102; BL 23000.

19. *Memoirs of William Hickey*, ed. Quennell, P.

20. Gilbert, R., ELHS NL 51, 1984, 5.

21. Parry, J.D., *The Coast of Sussex*, 1833.

22. Brunnarius, M., *Windmills of Sussex*, 1979. Hemming, P., *Windmills in Sussex*, 1936. Hodsoll, V.M., 'Mills of Eastbourne', ELHS NL 39, 1981, 11. Stevens, L., 'Some Windmill Sites in Friston and Eastbourne', SAC 120, 106-38. Stevens, L., 'Mills of the Eastbourne Borough Council Area', *Sussex Industrial History*, 27, 1997, 22-29.

23. In the 1990s Hodsoll, V., Milton, R., Putland, J. and Stevens, L. produced a version of the monuments and plates in the church, with brief descriptions and measurements, published by Webb, P. and Weir, N. of PBN as a fiche.

24. Wright, J.C., *Bygone Eastbourne*, 1902.

Three **Increased Prospects – 1850-1900, pp.35-60**

1. Sharpin, I.M., Williams, C.F., *A Postal History of Eastbourne*, 1972.

2. Hodsoll, V., ELHS NL 44, 1982, 5-8.

3. Needham, J., 'Frederick Gowland Hopkins', *Perspectives in Biology and Medicine* 6, 1962, 1.

4. Muncey, F., *Eastbourne Local Historian* [ELH 108], 1998, 9-16.

5. Brockhurst, E., *The Grand Parade Murder of 1860*, 1984.

6. *Eastbourne Gazette* 20/6/1866.

7. Allom, V.M., *Ex Oriente Salus: A Centenary History of Eastbourne College*, 1967.

8. Surtees, J., *Barracks workhouse and hospital St Mary's Eastbourne*, ELHS 1992.

9. Minutes of Eastbourne Union Guardians 21/12/1883, ESPRO (G 13/1a/15).

10. Oakum was the fibre teased from old hemp ropes and used for caulking boats.

11. Lester, A.M., 'The Evolution of St Mary's Hospital', *Eastbourne Medical Gazette*, 2, 1976, 34.

12. Graham, R.J., *Eastbourne Recollections*, 1888.

13. Giddey, W.D., *The Story of All Saints' Hospital*, 1974.

14. Pugh, P., *Grand Hotel*, 1987.

15. Milton, J.T., *History of the Royal Eastbourne Golf Club*, 1987.

16. Neville, G., *Religion and Society in Eastbourne 1735-1920*, 1982.

17. Pearson, J., *The Serpent and the Stag*, 1983.

Four **Solid Respectability 1900-1938, pp.61-95**

1. Milton, R., ELH 110, 1998, 13-17.

2. Surtees, J., *Beachy Head*, 1997.

3. It was alleged that the secret ingredient was a drop of black so that the colour could only be duplicated by coming back to Brewer's shop.

4. Ockenden, M., ELHS NL 74, 1989, 11.

5. Lewis, M., ELHS NL 37, 1980, 3-4.

6. Hodges, G., ELHS NL 16, 1975, 6.

7. Meek, G., *George Meek, Bath-Chairman, by himself*, 1910. Coxall, W., Griggs, C., *George Meek - Labouring Man: protege of H.G. Wells*, 1996.

8. Hodges, P.R., *Temples of Dreams*, 1994.

9. McMahon, L., Partridge, M., *A History of the Eastbourne Aviation Company*, 2000.

10. Letters to the local newspapers at this time bemoaned the fact that Eastbourne was 'not as select as it might be, for apartments are being let which are within the reach of the humblest, who are not all honest'.

11. Coverley, L.J., *History of Chelmsford Hall 1920-70*.

12. *The Times* 16/10/1917.

13. Elliston, R.A., *Eastbourne's Great War 1914-1918*, 1999.
14. Canon W.C. Streatfeild (1865-1929) was vicar of Eastbourne from 1911 to 1928; he died on a Lewes-Eastbourne train. His daughter, Mary Noel (1895-1986), wrote *Ballet Shoes* in 1936.
15. Browne, D.G., Tullett, T., *Bernard Spilsbury Life and Cases*, 1951. Bles, G., *The Trial of Patrick Mahon*, 1925.
16. Westcott, C., *Cricket at the Saffrons*, 2000.
17. Milton, J.T., *Origins of Eastbourne Street Names*, 1995.
18. Stevens, L., *The Vigil and the Morrow*, 1980.
19. The famous *Grand Hotel* chandelier has been moved to the Devonshire Park Theatre.
20. *Eastbourne Gazette* 5/4/1933.
21. *Municipal Eastbourne 1883-1933 (suppl. 1939)*, ed. Fovarque, H.W., 1939.
22. Brandon, P., Short, B., *The South East from AD 1000*, 1990.
23. *Eastbourne Herald*, 15/5/1937.
24. Reed, T., *The Fishermen and Boatmen of Eastbourne*, 1979.
25. Aspen, J.C., *A Municipal History of Eastbourne 1938-74*, 1979.

Five The Most Bombed Town on the South Coast, pp.96-110

1. Morris, J., Hendy, D., *The Story of the Eastbourne Lifeboats*, 1981.
2. Anderson shelters were named after Sir John Anderson, member of the War Cabinet, who is buried in All Saints' churchyard at West Dean. Nearby is the last resting place of F/O Hugh Ian Long RAF, died 20 April 1941, whose tombstone his widow Pam inscribed, 'One of our pilots is safe'.
3. Bobby's Stores advertised that they possessed one of the safest shelters in the town.
4. Chief Officer S.A. Phillips of the Fire Brigade was awarded the M.B.E., rescue squad members A.E. Blackmer, E.H. May, E.F. Stevens and E.L. Turney the G.M., and commendations went to Dr J. Fenton (MOH), Dr Barron, Mr Snowball, R.V. Harvey, S.N. Waymark, E.A. Homewood of the Fire Brigade, PC R.T. Jeffrey, and wardens H.M. Barnes and A.J. Barkham.
5. *Eastbourne Herald* 23/11/1940.
6. Humphrey, G., *Eastbourne at War*, 1998. Hardy, N.W., *Eastbourne 1939-45*, 1945.
7. Ashworth, C., *Action Stations No.9*, 115-18, 1985. Longstaff-Tyrrell, P., *Operation Cuckmere Haven*, 1997.
8. Ockenden, M., *Eastbourne Herald*, 19/8/1989.
9. Alfred Delles, a member of the 51 (Edelweiss) Fighter Squadron, confirms that the German aircraft used could not restart their engines in the air: 'They slowed the motors down on the approach and gave them full throttle after the raid before zigzagging over the sea to safety.' It is said that the rumour was not scotched because it gave encouragement to the populace if they thought the enemy had to resort to such 'scalded-cat' measures.
10. Of 4,963 Canadian troops who embarked for Dieppe, only 2,210 were withdrawn as planned.
11. Surtees, J., *Chaseley a Home from Home*, 1997.
12. Surtees, J., *The Princess Alice and other Eastbourne hospitals*, 1994.

Six Spotlight on a Changing Town, pp.111-27

1. Humphrey, G., *Wartime Eastbourne*, 1989. Sussex Express and County Herald, *The War in Sussex*, 1945.
2. Kefford, W.H., 'The Tech., a personal account', ELHS NL 76, 1990, 9-19.
3. Webb, P., *Cavendish Hotel Eastbourne*, 1998.
4. Harley, R.J., *Seaton and Eastbourne Tramways*, 1996.
5. *Eastbourne Herald* 20/2/1993, *Eastbourne Gazette* 17/2/1993.
6. *Eastbourne Herald Chronicle* 4/8/1951.
7. Surtees, J., *The Strange Case of Dr Bodkin Adams*, 2000.
8. *Eastbourne Gazette* 21/1/1959.
9. *Eastbourne Gazette* 14/9/1977, *Eastbourne Herald* 22/10/1977.
10. Guise, S., *The Great Redoubt*, 1979.
11. Thomas, E., *The Playhouse on the Park*, 1997.
12. Eastbourne Borough Council, *Roller Skates and Rackets*, 1999.
13. *Eastbourne Herald* 1/2/2002.

Index

References which relate to illustrations only are given in **bold**.

Adams, Dr Bodkin, 86, 117, **118**
Adams, Rev. Edward, 45
Agent to the Duke, 36, 52, 58, 76
Agricultural Show, 74
Air crash, 72, **91**, 96, 98, 108, **117**
Air raids, 96, 98-110, 130
Albert Parade, **82**
Albion Hotel, 14, **16**, 35, 52
Aldro School, 80, 98
Alfred, King, 22
Allchorn boats, **42**, **89**, **93,** 113
All Saints' Hospital, **47**, 49, 78, 104,
    118
All Souls' Church, 51
Amers, Capt. Henry, 80
Anderitum (Pevensey), 21
Apps, Stanley, 105-6
Araluen, 45
Ariadne, HMS, torpedoed, 78
Armada, Spanish, 27
Arndale Centre, 124-5
Artisans' Dwelling Co., 51
Attwell, Mabel Lucie, **73**
Austen, Jane, 10
Australian POWs, 110
Avenue, The, 44, 107
Aviation Company, 71-2, 75, 83

Badlesmere, Bartholomew de, 25
Ballast Line, 44, 81
bandstands, 61, **63**, **92**
Barnhill, SS, bombing, 96, **97**
barracks, 4, **6**, 11
bathing, 3, **59**, 60, 83-4, 97, 122
bathing huts, **4**, **59**
baths, 2, 24, 49, 66,
Beachy Head, 3, **12**, **20**, 29, **62**, **87**,
    100, **104**, **109**, **117**, 123
Beachy Head, Battle of, 28, 129
Beachy Head lighthouse, 61, **62**
Beaker People, **21**
Beckett family, 49
Bedford well, 36
Bell, Rt Rev. George, 91, 109
Belle Tout cliff shaft, **21**
Belle Tout lighthouse, **12**, 61, 90
bells, church, 12, 33, 52
Berry, James, 35-6, 41
Bennett, William Sterndale, 49

Bicycle Club, 50
Bindon, Stephen, 39
Birds Eye factory, **114**
Birling Gap, 2, 17
Black Death, *see* Plague
Black Hole of Calcutta, 32
Blackout, 96, **105**, 110
Blériot's monoplane, 72
Board of Ordnance, 4, 8
Bobby & Co., **74**
Bomb Alley, 104, 110
Borough Council, 52
Boult, John, 28
Bourne, first mention, 23
Bourne Place, **2**, 26, 29
Bourne Stream, **11**, **24**
bowling, 59, 87
Bradford family, 37, 123
Breweries, 29, 39, 41, 125
Brewer's, paints, 66, 129
bribery, 88
Broadbourne, **24**
Brodie family, 12, 45, **46**
Brodie Hall Infants' School, **40**
Brodie, Rev. Dr Alexander, 8-9, 11-12
Bronze-Age artefacts, 19, **21**
Brooke, Rupert, **73**
Browne, H.R., **38**
Browne, Rev. Edwin, 80
Bruyéres, Mr., 2
Bullock Down, 19, 21, 23, 39
Bungalow Stores **82**
Burlington, Blanche, Countess, **46**
Burlington, William, 2nd Earl, **5**, 14,
    35-6
Burlington Hotel, **35**, 43, 84, 100
Burnt Cottage, **9**
Burton family, 26
bus service, **65**, 76-7, 113
Busby, Frank, 96

cabmen's shelter, **72**
Caen stone, 24, 32
Caffyn's, **40**, 61, 63, **64**, 65, 79, 87,
    110, 122
Campbell, Colen, 29
Campbell's boats, **92**
Camden, William, 27
Canute, King, 23

Carnival, 118
Carpet Gardens, 35, 105, **122**
Carroll, Lewis, Rev. C.L. Dodgson, **40**,
    56
Castlereagh, Lord, 6
Cavalry (Horse) Barracks, 4, **5**
Cavalry Command Depôt, 77
Cavendish family, 12, 18, 60
Cavendish Hotel, 14, 49, 104-5
Cavendish, Lord George Henry, 4, **5**, 8
Cavendish, Major Hon. George, 8
Cavendish Place, 35
celebrations, 59, 89-90, 93-4, 115
cellars, **33-4**
Census, 18, 114
Central Military Hospital, 77, **79**
Chambers, G.F., 55
Chapman's tours, 81, 128
Charlwood's, jewellers, 52
Christ Church, **40**, 126
cinemas, 71-2, 85
Civil War, 27-8
Classis Britannica, 19
Claremont Hotel, 43
Clarke, D.A., 45
Clarke, Edward Daniel, 29
Cliff Cottage, 14
Clifton House School, 48, 52
coach tours, 81, 115
coal merchants, 37, 123
Coast Blockade, 10
Coastguards, **9**, 10-11, 14, 61, **62**
Coates, Eric, 80
Coles, J.H. Campion, 37, **43**
College, Eastbourne, 37, 44, 48, 77,
    104, 112
collier brigs, 16, 78
Colstock's Farm, **47**, 80
Commercial Hotel (Diplock's), 39
Commissioners of the Levels, 25
Compton, Lady Elizabeth, 2, **5**, 8
Compton Place, **2**, 26, 29, 39, **113**
Compton Place Lodge, **27**
confectioners, 89, 122
conference trade, 86, 115
Congress Theatre, **120**
Cook family, 38
Cooper, Robert, 37
Cooper's Brewery, 29

131

Cornfield Terrace, 37
Count of the Saxon Shore, 21
Crake, Rev. Edward, 48
Crematorium, 119
cricket, 39, 54, 72, 85
Crowden, Rev. Charles, 48
Crowlink, 10, 31
Crumbles, 4, 18, 25, 81-2
Crumbles Tramway, 115, **116**
Cumberland, Duke of, 6
Cumberland Hotel, 45
Currey, Henry, 36-7, 48-50
Customs and Excise, 10, 30-1
Customs House, 30

Danish invasion, 22, 23
Darwin, Charles, 18
Davies Gilbert family, 9, 12, 18, 27,
　43-4, 52, 73-4
de Roos, Lord William, 25
de Walden, Lady Lucy Joan, **48**
de Walden House, 48
Debussy, Claude Achille, 66
Dental Practice Agency, 50, 113-4
Devonshire, 3rd Earl of, 28
Devonshire, 7th Duke of, 36, 43, **44**,
　45, 49, 52, 57
Devonshire, 8th Duke of, 60-1, 66, 71
Devonshire, 9th Duke of, 71
Devonshire, 10th Duke of, 114
Devonshire, 11th Duke of, 104, 114,
　127
Devonshire Park & Baths, 49, 60, 71-2,
　86, 126
Devonshire Place, **36**
Diana, Princess, **126**
Dickens, Charles, 14
Dicker's Stores, 58
Diplock, Caleb, 39, 41
Diplock, Caleb jnr, 41, 91
'Dippers', **4**
District General Hospital, 124
Dolphin Court, **47**
Domesday Book, 24
dovecote, medieval, 31
Downland purchase, 86, **87**
Downs of Sussex, 29
Downs School, 80
Droveways, 25
Dunkirk survivors, **98**

Earp's Folly (Cliffe House), **44**
Eastbourne Chronicle/Herald, 39, 98
Eastbourne College of Arts and
　Technology (ECAT), 112-13
Eastbourne Gazette, 39, 49, 78, 98
Eastbourne Temperance Building
　Society, 51
East Dean, 2
Edgmond Hall, 3, 31
Edward, the Confessor, 23-4
Edward VII, 39, **64**, **68**
Egg, Augustus, 14

elections, 53, 88
Electric Light Co., 52, 61
Elgar, Sir Edward, 80
Elliott's Stores, 58
emigration, 13
Engels, Friedrich, 58
Erridge family, 27, 53
Esperance Hospital, 78
Evacuation, 96, 98, 110
Evenden, Henry, 38
'Eyes', 22

farming, 18-19, 24-6, 93, 114
Fair, 25-6
Farhill, Mr., 2
fever hospital (Downside), **68**
Field House, 35
Figg Map, **5**
Finch, Lady Charlotte, 1-2
Fire Brigade, 69-70, 107, 123
Fisher family, **7**
Fisher, Rev. John, 2
fishing, 16, 27, 52-3, 94
flints, **26**, 27, 32, **46**
football, 52, 80, 122
Ford, Louis G., **74**, 118
Ford, Capt. W.H., 6
Forster, E.M., 52
Fovargue, H.W., 94
Fowler, Frederick Bernard, **71**, 72
Francis, Richard and William, 39, 78
Freeman Thomas family, 4, 12, 16, 63
French Revolution, 3
Friston Place, 27
Fuller, 'Mad Jack', 12

Gas Company, 37, 44
Gibbs, Robert, 2
Giddy, Davies 12
Gilbert family (*see also* Davies Gilbert):
　Charles, 4, 34; John Davies, 14, 17;
　Mary Ann, 12; Nicholas, 5, 12;
　Peter and Douglas, 48
Gilbert Arms (*Squirrel*), 16, **17-18**, 44
Gildredge/Gilbert Manor House, 3, 12,
　27, 34
Gildredge Hotel, 45
Gildredge Park, 83, 105
Girls' High School, 94, 115
Goffs, The, **24**
Goldfinch, Capt. Henry, 8
golf, 54, 59-60, 63, 67, 70, 87, 93, 107
Gore Farmhouse, 9
Gorringe, John P, **18**
Gosden, John, 37, **43**
Gowland, Thomas Stafford, 42
Grace, W.G., 39
Graf Zeppelin visit, **90**
Graham family, 11, 48
Grand Hotel, 50, 57, 66, 72, 78, 96, 111
Grand Parade, 35, 42-3, 78, 84
Greensand, 19, 32, 35
Greys, The, 28

Grose, Francis, **6**
Guardians of the Poor, 13
Guides to Eastbourne, 2, 128
Guilds **25**, 31, **33**
Guinness, Sir Alec, 48

Haine family, **7**
Hall, Wilhelmina Brodie, 52
Hamel, Gustav, **71**
Hampden Park, 63, 84, **85**
Harding, Sir Charles, 79
Harling, Peggy, 101
Hartfield Farm, **17-8**
Hayman, Dr Charles, 41, **43**, 44
Heatherly, John, **3**, 11
Heathy Brow, 19
Helen Garden, 89
Herstmonceux Castle, 2
Hickey, William, 29, 34
Hide family, 27
Hill, George, 111
Hill, Sir Rowland, 52
Hillcote School, 80, 119
hockey, 80
Holy Trinity Church/School, **15**, 47
Holywell Italian Garden, 65-6
Home Fleet visit, 74
Home Guard, **99**
Homewood, Harry, 102
Hook, Theodore Edward, 14
Hopkins, Frederick, 42
Hopkins, Frederick Gowland, **41**, 42
Hopley, Thomas, 42-3
Hounsom, J.A., 69-70
How, Thomas, 8
Hudson, Ann, 4
Huggett, Alec, 96, 105
Hunt, Holman, 14
hunting, 57
Hurst, William, 29
Hurst's Cottages, 10
Hutments, The, 80, **82**
Huxley, Thomas Henry, 58

Indian Pavilion, 49, 88, **120**
industrial estates, 115
Influenza pandemic, 78-9
Invalids resort, 41
Iron Age: fields, 19; Hallstatt urn, **21**

Jazz Age, 80, **83**
Jenkie's band, 80
Jesus House **25**, 124
Jewell, Charles, 74, 76
Johnson, Amy, 88, **91**

Kaye, Emily Beilby, 82, **84**
Kinburn House/*Railway Hotel*, 37, 44, 87
King, Father Charles Patrick, 45

Ladies' College, 48
Lamb, Charles, 10
Lamb Inn, **3**, 26, 29, 34,

Langney, 43, 94, 121
Langney Forts, 4, 10
Lansdowne Hotel, 104
Larkfield House, 48
Larkin's Field, 45, 80
Lavis, G. & R., 42
Lawns, The, 28
LB&SC Railway, 17, 37, 61
Leaf Hospital, 78
Lear, Edward, 49
Letheren Place, **5**
Library, **10**, 11, 42, 59, 66, 107, **121**, 122
licence plates, **56**
Lieutenancy Records, 4, 6
lifeboats, 12, 52, **58**, 93, 96-7
Lind, Jenny, **14**
Links, 39, 54
Links School, 66-7, **68**
Lion Steam Brewery, 39, **41**
Llewellyn, Walter & Sons, 61
Local Board, 39, 55
London House, 39
Lords of the Manor, 4, 12, 18, 73
Lowther's Lambs, 77
Lushington, Henry, **32**
Lushington, Rev. Dr Henry, **32**, 33

Magistrates, 18, 48
Manor of Bourne, 26
Marine Parade, **16**, 18, 35
Market, 25, 53
Martello Towers, **4**, 6, **7**, 10
Martin, Mark, 61, 71
Marx, Karl, 52
Maternity Home, 76, 80, 115
Maynard, Edward, 37, 41
Meads, **3**, 36, 40, **47**, **48**, 70,
Meek, George, 52, 71
Merchant, H.B., 37
Methodist Chapel, 9, 73-4
Military funerals, 78
Militia, 4, 6, **8**
Miller, Glenn, 109
mills, 31, 129
Minstrel concert parties, 57
Model Village, 115, **116**, **119**
Moira House School, 50, 112
monasteries, dissolution, 26
Morris, Ebenezer, 37, **40**
Morris, James Berry, 14
Mortain, Robert Count of, 23-5
Mortimer, John Hamilton, 29
Motcombe pond, **24**
motor cars, 63, **64**, 65, 87, 104
Munro, Irene, 81
murders, 42-3, 73, 81-2, **84**
Musical Festival, 80

Napoleon, 6, 11
Neville House School, 90, 112
New College, 49
New Inn, 34

Nobel Laureates **41**, **118**
Norden, John 27
Nympha Americana, **28**
oakum, 47
Oates, Capt. Lawrence, 73
Ocklynge Junior School, 9
Old Town, **13**
Old Town Brewery, 29
Operatic and Dramatic Society, 66
Orchestras, **49**, 80, 95
Ordnance Yard, 4, 10, 30, 70, 75, 79, 118
Our Lady of Ransom Church, 61
Oxford, Earl and Countess of, 29

Palm Court Orchestra, 86-7
Parades, 52, 58-60
Parish Registers, 28
Parker Manor, 12, 27
Parker, Sir Thomas, 27
Parsons, Ron, **123**, 127
Peerless, James, 37, 41, 45, **53**
Pett, George, **9**
Pevensey Castle, 2
Philby, Kim, 80
photographers, 42
piano shops, 85-6
Pier, 37, 48, 61, 73, 98, 111, 123
Pierrot shows, 57, 60, **70**
Pilgrims, 33
Pillory Green, 31
Pitman, Rev. Thomas, **15**, **43**, 54
Pitt, William, 4, 6
Plague, 26-7
Pocock, Rev. Dr Richard, 29
Polegate, 17, 78, 97
Police, 18, 57-8, **95,** 123
Poor Rates, 14
population, 18, 37, 57, 98, 114
postal services, 8, 38-9, **74**
postbox, oldest, 38
Potts, Jane, 67, **68**
Powell, Sandy, 111-12
Pre-fabs, 111
Preventive Waterguard, 10
Prince Edward's visit, 2
Prince of Wales (Edward VIII), 88, **91**
Princes Park, 83
Princess Alice Hospital, 37, **51**, **64**, 73, 88
Princess Alice tree, **38**, 81

Queen Alexandra Cottage Homes, 66
Queen's Hotel, 50

Race Course, 39
railway, 17, 35, 37, 90
railway station, 16, 37, 43-4, **54**, 90, 98, 119
Ranny's School, 70, 98, 118
rationing, wartime, 78, 104
Ratton Manor, 12
Ravilious, Eric, 105

Rector of Eastbourne, 24-5, 31
Rectory Manor Parsonage barn and farm, **15**, 32
Red Cross Hospitals, 75-6
Redoubt Fortress, 6, 83, 113, 119
Regatta, 39
Riding School, 85
Robey, George, 77
Roborough School, 48
Roman artefacts, 19, 21, **22**, **23**, 24, 128
Rose, Arthur Clarkson, 75, 98
Rose Cottage, **11**
Round House, 4, 21, 35
Royer, James, 2
Rube family, 70, 117
rugby, 115
Rush, A.E., 105
Russell, Dr Richard, 1, 3

Saffrons sports ground, 54, 85, 110
St Aidan's Church, 73-4
St Andrew's School, Meads, **47**, 80, 112
St Anne's Church, 73, 106, 115
St Bede's School, 63, 112
St Cyprian's School, 67, 69
St Elisabeth's Church, 91
St Gregory's Chapel, **25**
St John's Church, **44**, 45, 105, 117
St Luke's Children's Hospital, **47**
St Mary's Church, **6, 12**, 24-5, 31, **32**, 33
St Mary's Girls' School, 9
St Mary's Hospital, **6**, 84, 97, 110, 115
St Mary's Church School, 9, 47
St Saviour's Church, **44**, 45
St Wilfrid, 22
St Winifred's School, 3
Salmon, David, **38**
Salvation Army, 55, 88
Sapseid, Cecil and his band, **83**
Sayer's boats, 42
Saxon church, 23, 32
Saxon invasion, 21-2
Saxon spearhead and brooches, **23**
Scarlet fever epidemic, 43
schools, 3, 13, 37, 42, **46**, 47-8, 55, 63, 80, 94, 112, 115
Scottish Pipe Band, 53
Seaford School House, 13
seafront, **42**, **112**
Seahouses, 1, **3-4**, 18, 29
seawall, 35, 52
Selwyn, John 27
sewage outfall, **43**, 122
Shady Lane (Trinity Trees), 1
Shaw, George Bernard, **73**
sheep farming, 26
Sheepwash, **3**, **11**, **24**, 28, 66
Shinewater, Bronze-Age settlement, **21**
shipwrecks, **28**, 29, **117**, 123
Sims, George Robert, 47
Smallpox Hospital, 58, 104

Smith, Dr William Abbott, 41
smuggling, **9**, 10, 30-1, 128
'Snoot Parade', 61, 95
Snowball, L.A.H., 101, 104, 108-9
Soddy, Frederick, **118**
Soldiers' and Sailors' Home, 74
Southbourne, 1, **3**
South Cliff Tower, 119, 121
Southdown Bus Station, **41**
Southfield Lodge, 3
Sovereign Centre/Harbour, 125-6
Spencer Compton, **5**, 27, 29
Spilsbury, Sir Bernard, 82
statues, **36**, 61
Stella Maris Church, 45
Stevens, Leonard, 39
Stone-Age axes and scraper, 19
Streatfeild, Canon W., 79
Street, G.E., 45
Sub-postmaster, first, 8
Suffragettes, 73
Summerdown Camp, 76
sunshine, **62**, 72
Sussex Weekly Advertiser, 4, 6
Sutton, Henry, 44-5

Taylor, Sir Charles, 88, 96
Teale, Major Edward, 78
Technical Institute, 66, **67**, 107
telephones, 52, 83, 123
Tennyson, Lord Alfred, **14**
Terminus Road, 17
Thames, **12**

Theatres, **7**, 49, 61, 88, 98, 121, 125
Thomas, *see* Freeman Thomas
Thurlow, Edward Baron, 29
Titanic memorial, 73
Town Clerk, 37
Town Hall, 48, 53-4
Towner Art Gallery & Museum, **22**, 34, 83
Towner, John Chisholm, 83
Trafalgar, Battle of, 8
transportation for smuggling, 10
Treats, 55, 74
Trevin Towers, 114
Tuberculosis Hospital (Gildredge), 74-5
Tutors to the Prince, 2
Twiss, Brig.-General, 6

U-boats, 78, **100**, 105
Uncle Bertie's Hour, 115
unemployed, 82-3, 87
Upperton Farm, **18**
Upperton Road, 44, **123**

VC awards, 48, 76-7
venereal diseases clinic, 78
Vestry Hall, **39**, 48
Vicars of Eastbourne, 8, **15**, 28
Victoria Place, 17, 35
Vidler, Albert, 42
Vine, Henry, 37
visitors, famous, 9, 10, 14, 18, 49, 52, 58, 66, 73, 90, 126-7

Walker, Edward, **45**
Wallis, G.A., 36, **43**, 49, 52, 54, 58-9
Walls, Inspector A., murder of, 73
Walter, John, 12
War Memorials, 79, **81**, **111**, **124**
Watch House, 10, 14
Watch Tower, **62**
Water Company, 36, **48**
Water Supply, 24, 35-6
Waterworks Act, 36
Waterworks Road, 36, 109
Western Lawns, 61, 78
Wheatears, 28, 29
Whelpton, Rev. H.R., **44**
Whelpton's pills, 45
Whitley, Nicholas and Michell, 44
Wilberforce, William, 10
Wilkes, Mr and Mrs Vaughan, 67, 69
Willard family, 1, 9, **22**, 28, 48
William the Conqueror, 23
Willoughby, Dr W.G., 80
Wilson family, 27, 28, 29
windmills, *see* mills
Winter Garden, 49, 107
Wish Tower, **4**, 6, **56**, **120**
Wood, Ald. Percy, 80, 118
Wood, Rev. James Russell, 44
Workhouse, Union, **6**, 11, 13, **46**, 47, 77, 84

YMCA, 76, 86, 119
Ye Rising Sun, 52
York House Hotel, **60**